ENDORSEMENTS

"Property Decisions is a thoughtful, user-friendly guide that every family should use. It offers a host of questions that families should discuss and evaluate to try to avoid the contentious disputes that often follow the death of a loved one. As a trust litigator who has handled hundreds of such cases, I can assure every family that you don't want the delay, expense, and turmoil of a protracted family fight."

—Margery S. Bronster, Former Attorney General, State of Hawaii

Founding Partner Bronster Fujichaku Robbins, Law Firm

"Property Decisions reminds us that real estate is never just about property. It is about people, family, and the choices we make when it matters most. This book provides the clarity families need to make decisions with confidence and unity."

—Patsy K. Saiki, Vice President – Division | State Manager, First American Title Company

"As a Certified Financial Planner I have been doing retirement and long term care planning for the past 40 years. I believe there are no accidents, people who succeed in life are proactive, intentional, and have a plan. To bring their dreams to life they need a good plan and good execution both. This book gives the reader information, tools and a roadmap to do this."

—Michael W.K. Yee, Private Wealth Advisor,
A financial advisory practice of Amerprise
Financial Services, LLC

"I have been a probate and elder law attorney in Hawaii for decades. Dan and his team were years ahead of his colleagues in foreseeing the surging aging-related need for real estate transactions of our kupuna. It is because of this foresight, combined with the tireless efforts of Dan and his entire team to go above and beyond what most realtors do, that I have worked with him on the many real property transactions I have handled in my practice, and I highly recommend that you do as well. The book is based on their business model and serves as a

valuable roadmap for addressing aging-related needs. A must read."

—Chris Dias, Attorney at Law Inc.

"This book helps the patriarchs and matriarchs in a family communicate, connect, and avoid conflict on life's most awkward conversations… death, taxes, and the transfer of wealth. It will help you to create a living legacy while you're alive, not just leave one after you're gone."

—Scott Hogle, President iHeartMedia Honolulu & Bestselling Author PERSUADE

"Property Decisions is a must-read for anyone who owns property. Dan generously shares his hard-earned insights on real estate decision-making—wisdom that not only helps protect a family's wealth, but also preserves relationships along the way."

—Glenn Young, MD

"People don't plan to fail, but they fail to plan"

"What a great topic and book that the Iharas created. We are facing a silver tsunami and as an

insurance agent, we are advising and assisting these families transfer homes properly. Many don't realize that once your parents leave us, the financial interest changes. Many times, people don't let the insurance companies know and this could impact coverage. Vacant homes are also another hazard. The Ihara's spoke about houses that sit vacant. What many don't know is that a squatter that enters the home and starts a fire could potential become the responsibility of the owner. This book covers many important topics that the next generation needs to understand as trustees and future owners. What I really liked is that there are professionals out there that could not only make you money on an inherited property but maximizing what you get from the right professionals caught my eye. Team up with a team that will look out for your best interest. It's a must read. I hope you enjoy this as much as I did."

—Bradley Maruyama,
20 Year Allstate Insurance Agent

"Seeing how money (real estate in particular) can tear apart families, especially when parents work so

hard to leave a legacy for their children, "Property Decisions" is essential for keeping the peace and dreams alive for parents wishing to leave a lasting legacy that will provide the foundation for many generations to come."

—Dr. Shaun Ohira, Owner, Hawaii Elite Chiropractic

"We are in the middle of the greatest wealth transfer in history. Property Decisions is a critical resource for anyone managing estate assets, giving you smart and sound advice to make the best decisions for your family and your finances."

—Amanda Butterfield, Director of Partnerships, The Institute for Luxury Home Marketing

"Dan is an expert in working with elderly clients and their heirs. In his book Property Decisions, he gives practical, real life examples of how to navigate complex sales that other agents walk away from. He takes the guesswork out and shows you how to execute with care and professionalism. Due to the aging demographic of so many homeowners in

America, this book is super timely for those that want to work with the segment of the population with the most amount of real estate assets."

—Scott Ostrode, Owner,
Team Ostrode Properties

PROPERTY DECISIONS

Avoid Painful Taxes & Family Disputes
to Build a Legacy That Lasts

DAN & JULIE IHARA

Property Decisions: Avoid Painful Taxes & Family Disputes to Build a Legacy That Lasts

Written by Dan & Julie Ihara

to their individual circumstances. Laws, regulations, and financial practices vary across countries, states, and regions. Market conditions, returns, and outcomes will differ over time and cannot be guaranteed. While every effort has been made to provide accurate and timely information at the time of writing, we make no representations or warranties regarding completeness, accuracy, or applicability. We are not making any official legal or financial recommendations. The examples, figures, and principles presented herein are for illustrative and educational purposes only. Any decisions you make are solely your responsibility.

DEDICATION

To our parents, our children, and every family standing at a crossroads.

Your love, your courage, and your desire to "do the right thing" inspired every page of this book.

May these questions guide you.
May these stories encourage you.

And may your decisions bless the ones you love—
not just today, but for generations to come.

FREE BONUS FOR READERS

We created a companion training that walks you through the key strategies in this book — step by step. It's our gift to you.

Scan below or visit free.danihara.com

TABLE OF CONTENTS

FOREWORD
BY GARY KELLER

Most people think real estate is about property. It isn't. It's about people.

Behind every piece of property is a story. A story of work and dreams, of sacrifice and success, and of even disappointment. For almost five decades, I've had a front-row seat to those stories. I've watched families use real estate to build extraordinary wealth and security. I've also seen that same wealth create tension, confusion, and division when clarity and communication were missing.

Buying and selling property is the easy part. What comes next is harder. Deciding what to do with it. How to manage it. How to share it, and ultimately, how to pass it on in a way that strengthens relationships instead of straining them.

That's why this book matters.

What families are often missing isn't effort or good intentions. They're missing a plan. A clear framework. A way to see the whole picture so they can make confident decisions together. This book provides exactly that. It brings structure to complexity and replaces uncertainty with understanding.

What impressed me most as I read these pages is how seamlessly the authors connect the practical with the personal. They address the realities of taxes, cash flow, legal structures, and strategy while never losing sight of what truly matters. Love. Trust. Legacy. Family. That balance is rare, and it's essential.

One idea kept coming back to me as I read. Clarity really is power.

When people understand their situation clearly, they stop reacting and start making decisions with intention instead of emotion. Families that gain clarity around their real estate don't just protect assets. They protect relationships. How?

They build legacies on purpose—not by default.

The planning framework introduced here does something very powerful. It takes what feels overwhelming and breaks it down into something simple, visual, and actionable. It turns confusion into confidence. Just as importantly, it turns silence into conversation. Honest, grounded conversations that hold families together across generations.

We're entering a period many call the "silver tsunami." The largest transfer of wealth in history. Without education and planning, that transfer can become a source of conflict and regret. But with the right tools, it can become one of the greatest blessings a family ever experiences.

This book is one of those tools.

It doesn't just teach strategy. It gives families a shared language. It's a roadmap for anyone who wants their real estate decisions to serve both their financial goals and their family's future.

The authors wrote this book for a simple but powerful reason: They care deeply about keeping families together. In a world where complexity often divides, this book does the opposite. It pulls everyone together, and in my experience, this is where all great legacies begin.

So, take a deep breath, open your mind, and start reading. What you'll find here isn't just advice. It's a blueprint. Not just for managing property, but for building purpose, generational wealth, and peace.

I can't think of anything more important than that.

Onward…

Gary Keller
Co-Founder & Executive Chairman of Keller Williams Realty International

PART 1

The Wake-Up Call

Introduction

Every morning, somewhere in America, a family is about to be torn apart.

And their being "'torn apart" doesn't always look as dramatic as you may assume. Often, it's far quieter and even more devastating.

When a family is torn apart, they stop celebrating holidays together. One child feels burdened, another feels forgotten, and both feel misunderstood. These family members build resentment that slowly grows in the silence because no one was brave enough, or guided enough, to start the conversations that would have protected their relationships.

And sadly, the resentment could all be over a home. A property meant to hold love and memories, but instead becomes the thing that breaks a family open.

By the time you finish reading this page, a family across the country may have started arguing over a property their parents left behind. One sibling wants to keep it, another needs the money, and the third just wants it gone. What should have been a blessing becomes a battlefield.

We have seen this kind of family conflict thousands of times in the twenty years as real estate professionals. And this book exists to make sure your family is not next.

WHY THIS BOOK EXISTS

The purpose behind this book is fourfold, and all based on the fact that too many families are destroying themselves over something that could have been prevented.

This book exists because:

- 70% of families fight over real estate after their parents pass away.[1] This is becoming an epidemic of fractured relationships, loss

---

1 Roy WIlliams and Vic Preisser. *Preparing Heirs: Five Steps to a Successful Transition of Family Wealth and Values.* Robert D. Reed Publishers, 2003.

of wealth, and missed opportunities to build generational stability. In all fairness, these are not bad people. These brothers, sisters, aunts, and uncles are good family members who simply never had a plan.

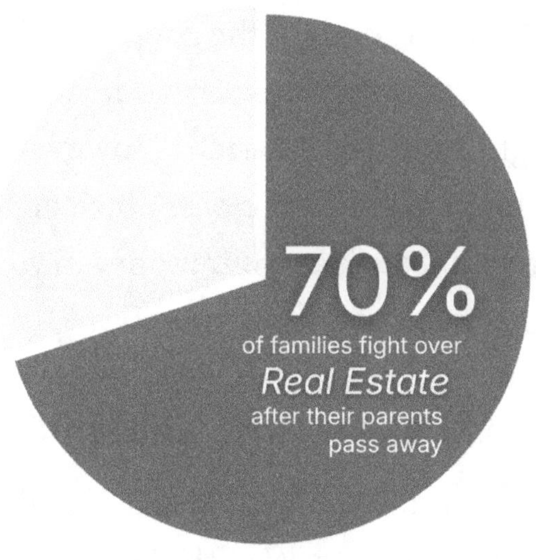

- The real estate industry has failed consumers. We have kept the most powerful wealth-building tools, like 1031 exchanges, locked away in professional circles. Meanwhile, people are losing hundreds of thousands of dollars to capital gains taxes simply because no one told them there was another way.

- Families are dealing with disputes that could have been avoided. The goal is to reach families before the crisis hits, not after the damage is done.

- Money is good for the good it does. But only if it actually gets to do good. When families fight, lawyers get rich. However, families who plan are able to pass down generational wealth. Let's keep your money in your family. This book will show you how.

WHO WE ARE AND WHY WE WROTE THIS BOOK

We're Dan and Julie Ihara, husband and wife, and certifiedReal Estate Wealth Advisors based in Hawaii.

For the past two decades, we've worked with families navigating the most emotional and financially significant decisions of their lives. We've seen what works, and we've seen what tears families apart.

We've also been through these emotional and financial hurdles ourselves, not just as advisors helping other families, but as sons and daughters watching our own parents age.

I'm the youngest of six siblings. When my parents' health started declining, the family fractured over what to do. Everyone had an opinion, but no one had a framework. The tension that followed could have been avoided with one honest conversation years earlier.

Julie walked a similar road, advocating for her mother's care and watching how quickly family dynamics shift when health changes the equation.

We wrote this book because we don't want your family to learn these lessons the hard way.

WHAT YOU WILL ACCOMPLISH BEFORE YOU EVEN FINISH THIS BOOK

The goal of this book is not to make you become a real estate expert. You have enough going on in your life. Rather, these pages will help you start to ask yourself the right questions.

Questions like: "Do I need the income from my investment property to sustain the life I want?" Or, "If money is good for the good it does, what good do I want my money to do?"

By the time you close this book, you will know exactly which questions matter most for your situation. Because people don't need someone to tell them what to do. There is enough of that in the world already. What they do need is someone to help them discover their options and ask the questions that lead to confident decisions.

To make that discovery process as clear as possible, this entire book is around three core insights.

THE THREE THINGS THAT WILL CHANGE YOUR OUTLOOK

If you only remember three things from this book, let them be these:

1. Real estate is wealth waiting to be unlocked. That lake house your grandparents built, the home where you raised your kids. Behind all

those memories is an asset worth money, but only when you treat it like one.

2. The biggest threat to generational wealth is not market crashes or interest rates. It's actually the lack of planning to prevent capital gains tax, estate tax, and family disputes. For some families, combined federal and state capital gains taxes can exceed 30%, and in some states reach as high as 37% for those who fail to plan ahead.[2]

3. You have more options than you think. Whether it is avoiding capital gains taxes, creating income streams, blessing your kids while you are still alive, or knowing where to go and how to pay for it when your current home no longer works for you, there are strategies available that most people never hear about

---

2 KDA Inc., "Capital Gains Tax in California: Why Most Investors Overpay (and How to Legally Cut Your 2025 Bill)," KDA Inc., August 10, 2025, https://kdainc.com/capital-gains-tax-in-california-why-most-investors-overpay-and-how-to-legally-cut-your-2025-bill/.

These three insights came from a fundamental shift in approach, and they are the same insights that will challenge your thinking in how you approach your real estate decisions.

HOW THIS APPROACH MADE ALL THE DIFFERENCE

Helping families ask the right questions shifted Julie and me from selling houses to preserving legacies.

Twenty years ago, we were just two REALTORS ® in the market. Today, our focus is on helping older adults transition to a living environment that works for them, preventing family disputes before they happen, helping people keep more of their money, and guiding families through the biggest financial decisions of their lives.

The difference comes from stopping the practice of telling people what to do and starting to ask them what matters most to them.

That shift in approach is exactly what you will discover in these pages.

OUR HIGHEST HOPE FOR YOU

When you finish this book, our hope is that you will look at your real estate as more than just buildings. These buildings are your opportunities to build wealth, take care of your family, and create a legacy that brings people together instead of being pulled at the seams.

Our hope is also that you will have the confidence to seek out a real wealth advisor who can help you turn these ideas into action. And most importantly, our hope is that your family will help change a statistic. Right now, 70% of families are torn apart by real estate decisions.[3] We're here to flip that story so that conflict can become clarity, resentment can give way to unity, and families can stay connected because they planned well. That's what we're fighting for.

But before we get to that point, let's be clear about who this book will help most.

---

3 Roy WIlliams and Vic Preisser. *Preparing Heirs: Five Steps to a Successful Transition of Family Wealth and Values.* Robert D. Reed Publishers, 2003.

WHO WE HELP AND HOW

This book helps real estate owners grow their assets, safeguard their wealth, and pass it on to the next generation so they can keep their families together and create lasting prosperity.

Maybe you are a baby boomer wondering what to do with the family home. It could be that you are an adult child watching your parents struggle with these decisions. Maybe you are an investor with a portfolio of properties, and it is time to pass it on. Or maybe you inherited property and do not know where to start. This book will give you the questions and framework you need to move forward with confidence.

Now, let's walk through exactly what to expect as we move through this journey together.

WHERE WE GO FROM HERE

Before you start thinking, "Is this just another real estate book?" we want to give you the simplest and straightforward answer...*no*.

Think of what you are about to read as a family preservation guide disguised as a wealth-building strategy.

First, you will see what is possible when families get this right. You will discover real case studies of people who avoided the 70% statistic and used their real estate to bring their families closer together while building lasting wealth.

After that, you will be able to identify exactly where you stand today. Through a series of assessments and questions, you will discover whether you are facing the same challenges that tear other families apart, and what specific steps you need to take based on your unique situation.

Next, you will walk through a complete framework for building, protecting, and passing on real estate wealth. You'll learn the process that the families we work with use every day, and when you're done, you'll know what questions to ask, which decisions to make, and how to find the professions you will need on your team.

Finally, you will focus on implementation. By the end of this book, you will know exactly what actions to take first, how to have those difficult family conversations, and where to get help when you need it.

If you are worried about needing to become an expert in 1031 exchanges or memorizing tax codes, wipe that worry away because this will not be the case for you. All you need to understand are your options. From there, you can be knowledgeable enough about the right questions to ask the right professionals.

At the end of this book, you will have an opportunity to join our Real Estate Wealth Hive, a community where consumers and professionals come together to share knowledge and solve problems. But for now, all I am asking is that you keep reading.

Because you will likely know someone out there who could have used this information last year. Do not let that family be yours.

It is time to start asking better questions. Let's begin.

With love, respect and purpose,
Dan and Julie Ihara

BEFORE YOU TURN THE PAGE

This book will give you the questions. But if you want
to go deeper and see these strategies in action,
we've put together a free training just
for readers of this book.

It picks up right where these pages leave off.

Scan below or visit free.danihara.com

CHAPTER 1

What's Possible–Real Stories of Family Success

*"The best time to plant a tree was 20 years ago.
The second best time is now."*
—Chinese Proverb

Imagine walking into a retirement community and seeing a seventy-eight-year-old woman surrounded by friends, laughing over afternoon tea, and completely at peace, knowing her family's future is secure.

This woman does not worry about being a burden to her family. She does not lie awake wondering if her money will last. When she passes away, her children will not be meeting with lawyers about property disputes. Instead, they will be celebrating a legacy that brought them closer together instead of tearing them apart.

That peace is what happens when families understand how to build, protect, and pass on real estate wealth the right way.

For the past twenty years, we've witnessed what happens when families plan, and what happens when they don't. We have been in rooms where siblings refuse to speak to each other over a house their parents left behind. But we've also witnessed families who stay connected and use their real estate to create opportunities that support the family for the long run.

If you are thinking that these radically opposite realities have anything to do with intelligence, degrees, luck, inheritance size, or market timing, the truth is, they don't. The difference is understanding that real estate is a wealth-building tool that, when handled correctly, can transform multiple generations. But what does this look like in practice?

WHAT IF THERE'S ANOTHER WAY?

Twenty years ago, we met Hilda, who became not only our lovely client, but also a defining example of how families can transform their circumstances through strategic real estate planning.

However, Hilda did not start out in a good place. The floors in her home were not visible. There were newspapers stacked to the ceiling, boxes everywhere, and only a narrow trail from the door to the sink, the toilet, the bed, the couch in front of the TV, and the back to the door. Everything else had stuff on it.

Hilda had been trying to sell her home for a year with no success. She was a retired teacher with some health issues and was not able to move much physically. She knew she needed to move to a retirement community, but felt trapped by multiple overwhelming problems: too many accumulated belongings, deferred maintenance, termite damage, and concerns about the capital gains taxes she would face when selling. All of these factors led to an unsellable house.

Most real estate agents would have walked away. The house looked unsellable, and the tax situation seemed impossible to solve. But we had a different perspective.

We thought, what if there could be a solution to all three of Hilda's problems at once? What if there were a way to move forward without losing a massive chunk of wealth to taxes?

In those early days of our careers, twenty years ago, it was just Julie and me. We asked Hilda a simple question: "Would you like some help clearing up the house to improve its value?" She said yes. She didn't realize she had a problem with the way she was trying to sell her house, she just knew something wasn't working. So we brought in a forty-foot container and systematically cleared decades of Hilda's accumulated belongings. During that process, we discovered that Hilda had been renting out a downstairs unit, which meant her "primary residence" was actually a mixed-use property.

That small detail changed her situation completely.

Working with tax professionals, including the late, respected, and pioneering 1031 exchange attorney and CPA Walton Liu, our team structured what is called a mixed-use 1031 exchange. Hilda used IRC Section 121 to claim $250,000 in tax-free gains on her primary residence portion, while simultaneously deferring the remaining capital gains through a 1031 exchange on the investment portion.

The results included:

- elimination of capital gains taxes,
- generating $2,200 monthly income from the replacement investment property, and
- financial resources to cover her retirement community entrance fee (just north of a million dollars) and ongoing care costs.

The rental income from the investment property helped fund her monthly service fees at the retirement community, solving multiple problems simultaneously.

When Hilda first sat in that cluttered house, her situation felt impossible. But the right questions revealed options she didn't know existed. The heart of real estate planning is more than buying and selling properties; it's designing the life you want and positioning your assets to make it possible. And when families experience this kind of transformation, word spreads quickly.

THE RIPPLE EFFECT BEGINS

Word spread through Hilda's neighborhood. Over the next twelve months, we hosted open houses on that same hill every Sunday, and neighbors kept approaching us: "What did you do for Hilda? How did you do it? Can you help me?" We went from one listing to seven.

Each situation that people in our community brought to us was unique, but the pattern was consistent.

Once word of how we helped Hilda spread, a family of three brothers (in their sixties and seventies) came to a seminar we were hosting because they did not know what to do about their father's home. Their father was in his late eighties to nineties and getting frail. Since the early seventies, their dad had been building wealth. He owned fifteen properties scattered all over the country, some in Oahu and some elsewhere.

The challenge was clear: Dad wanted to make it easy for his kids and worried about them fighting when he was gone because there were too many decisions to make. He wanted to simplify life.

So what did we do? We helped them create a plan to defer capital gains tax, therefore maximizing their legacy. Through coordinated 1031 exchanges, we helped them trade five properties for one, multiple times, until fifteen scattered holdings became a simplified, manageable portfolio. An important note: This was a bit tricky since the timelines were all tied together, and we were dealing with agents in four states who were not experienced in the 1031 exchanges. This was the most stressful 1031 exchange we ever executed, but it worked. The family consolidated into fewer assets closer to home, all while deferring taxes.

The most meaningful outcome, though, was what they did for the next generation. One real estate exchange that this family of three brothers made specifically included a grandson who had been renting his entire life. In this transaction, they used a partial 1031 exchange. So one group of properties they sold was exchanged into an asset that could be co-owned with the grandson, and put a mortgage on that asset. That means that when his grandpa dies, the grandson will get that portion tax-free.

The three brothers went from potential conflict over complicated inheritances to grateful collaboration on a plan that blessed the next generation while they were alive to see it.

Dad later passed away, and the children and grandchildren were able to enjoy the benefits of his years of wealth building with no stress. At family parties, they now reminisce about how smart he was in building wealth and passing it on while he was alive.

What sets successful real estate families apart is that they understand that wealth is about strategic positioning for maximum impact across generations. The same principles that transformed this family's situation work for others as well.

WHEN THE APPROACH TRANSFORMS THE PRACTICE

The question-based approach we used with both Hilda and the three brothers who came to visit Julie and me changed their outcomes and revamped how we practice real estate.

We didn't just transform these families' lives. We transformed our own.

The old way of doing real estate meant working twelve-hour days, staying up until 11:00 p.m., putting together educational packets, and touching every single client transaction personally. The stress was constant, and vacation meant working from the ski slopes with a phone pressed to our ears while the kids waited. It wasn't until we saw the look on our boys' eyes and heard their words, "I thought this was our vacation," that we realized something had to change.

The solution that worked for Hilda and the brothers worked for our business too. By building systems around strategic questioning rather than transactional selling, we created a consultative approach that builds lifetime plans using questions to unlock opportunities and imagination.

Most importantly, we can focus on what matters most: God, family, and work—in that order. We get to watch every sunrise and sunset, surf every day, and still help families across the country avoid the 70% statistic. We can truly say we are blessed beyond belief.

With our consultative approach, we can reshape how families think about wealth, the manner in which professionals serve clients, and the way business can serve life rather than consume it.

This approach transformed the entire practice of real estate wealth advising. The same principles that revolutionized these families' situations (and our own) work for others as well.

BEYOND INDIVIDUAL SUCCESS

You may think that these are isolated victories, but the truth is, they're not. The principles that created these outcomes have been tested across thousands of families for over two decades. When implemented correctly, they consistently produce three measurable benefits:

- The first is financial freedom through asset optimization. Families we work with discover that underperforming real estate can be repositioned into higher-yield investments without triggering massive tax consequences. Instead of accepting whatever income their properties generate, they learn to measure performance like any other investment and make strategic moves to maximize returns.

- The second is family harmony through clear planning. Rather than leaving inheritance decisions to chance, our successful families create pre-inheritance plans that eliminate disputes before they start. Children understand their inheritance while parents are alive to explain the reasoning and ensure value.

- The third is peace of mind through professional guidance. Instead of hoping for the best, families we work with assemble teams of specialists who coordinate tax strategies, estate planning, and real estate transitions. They move from reactive crisis management to proactive wealth building.

While many families fight over real estate inheritance, families with clear real estate wealth plans report the opposite experience. Inheritance actually brings them closer together. So what creates this dramatic difference in outcomes?

THE STRATEGY THAT CHANGES THINGS

The strategy that creates these transformative results relies on a question-based approach rather than telling families what to do. Real Estate Wealth Advisors like us guide families through self-discovery processes that help them identify what matters most to them, then show them how their real estate can support those goals.

For example, successful advisors never tell someone whether to keep or sell an investment property. Instead, they ask: "Do you need the income from this property to sustain the lifestyle you desire?"

If the answer is yes, professionals analyze whether the property is performing at its highest potential and explore ways to optimize returns.

If the answer is no, they ask: "If you could bless your family today, while you're alive to see it, would you?"

That question opens entirely different possibilities—pre-inheritance planning, 1031 exchanges into properties better suited for the next generation, or repositioning assets to create educational funds for grandchildren.

Bottom line: Your real estate should serve your life goals, not dictate them.

Most people have their relationship with their real estate backwards. They own properties and assume they are stuck with whatever those properties provide. Successful families flip that dynamic. They decide what they want their wealth to accomplish, then strategically position their real estate to make it happen.

WHAT THIS MEANS FOR YOUR DAILY LIFE

Beyond preventing family disputes and preserving wealth, this questions-based real estate strategy changes how you wake up each morning—with clarity instead of worrying about what will happen to everything you have built.

Consider what happened to one of our previous clients, the only child of a widow who passed away. This son, already in his sixties or seventies with his own place to live, didn't know what to do with his mother's house, so he left it vacant.

Her son left it vacant so long that weeds started growing, and neighbors complained. He had to spend money to cut the grass and still kept his mother's belongings in the house because he did not know what to do with them. Eventually, some homeless people saw the vacant home and started living there.

The situation deteriorated until there was a fire, and his solution was to tear the house down entirely. Then, he had a vacant lot and *still* did not know what to do with it. He had to pay property taxes on a property with no income, and it remained a burden.

When he attended one of our seminars, he learned that he could sell his land, without tax consequences, by executing a 1031 exchange. Then, he could buy a condo. Before this, he did not have any idea what he could do with the house since he did not have the money to rebuild it, nor did he want to. We helped him sell the vacant lot and buy a condo to rent out, which generated him $2,400 monthly. In other words, we helped him unlock that wealth and reposition it from a burden into an income-producing asset, transforming his inheritance from a liability into a financial benefit.

The families we spoke about in this chapter did not need to become real estate experts. They simply needed to understand their options and work with Real Estate Wealth Advisors who could execute the strategies that aligned with their values and goals.

THE PATH FORWARD

Now, the thought of "get-rich-quick schemes" or complex financial maneuvers that only wealthy families can afford may come to mind at this point. Maybe everything we've discussed in this chapter is good to be true, right? Absolutely not. Families just like yours can achieve the same success. It simply starts with looking at your real estate through a more strategic lens.

What is required is not massive wealth or advanced financial education. You just need to be willing to ask better questions and seek professional guidance rather than hoping for the best.

The solution starts with understanding a simple truth: Real estate is wealth waiting to be unlocked. That house with doors and windows represents options, opportunities, and the ability to impact your family's future in ways you may not have considered.

Most importantly, the real estate strategies we laid out in this chapter are not ones that you implement once and forget about. They are part of an ongoing approach to wealth building that serves families across multiple generations. In fact, we now offer our clients Annual Real Estate Plan Reviews similar to a financial planner. We do this because we know life happens. Couples get married, children are born, family members pass away or move away, some get divorced, and the needs of the family change. Our clients appreciate revisiting their real estate wealth strategies so they can appropriately plan ahead versus reacting to life changes.

We do this work because we can empathize with and understand our clients' journeys through our own experiences. Julie and her siblings walked through the exhausting journey of caring for her mom and advocating for her mother's care, learning firsthand how overwhelming these transitions can be without a plan.

And in my own family, my mom began to fall repeatedly while my dad grew too frail to lift her anymore. Out of six kids, there were different perspectives and options of what to do next, and resentment began to build. Along with my siblings' varied opinions, my parents were not in agreement. In their seventies, my mom wanted to move to a retirement community, but my dad didn't. In their late eighties and early nineties, my dad wanted to move into a retirement community, and my mom didn't. By this time, my parents went through months of unnecessary danger and family tension that could have been avoided. That experience helped us understand how difficult aging and caring for parents can become. We believe this is why God had us meet and serve so many families, to help them ask those questions sooner, before the crisis hits.

When we have conversations with clients, we ask them to imagine their best life and describe what it looks like. Call us dreamers, but we believe that when you live an intentional life, your dreams can come true.

In the pages ahead, you will discover exactly how to assess your current situation, identify your biggest opportunities, and take the first steps toward creating your own family success story.

Your next question is whether you are ready to see your real estate as more than just property and start using it as a tool to create the life and legacy you actually want.

As we move forward together, remember that every family that has transformed their financial future started exactly where you are right now—with questions about what is possible and a willingness to explore options they had not considered before.

Let's discover what is possible for *your* family.

REALITY CHECK

Before diving deeper into the strategies that make these transformations possible, take a moment to honestly answer these three questions:

1. **Do you have a plan for what happens to each piece of real estate you own when you pass away?**

   ☐ Yes   ☐ No

2. **Do all your adult children know and understand what they will inherit and why?**

   ☐ Yes   ☐ No

3. **Can you calculate your potential capital gains tax liability if you sold your properties today?**

   ☐ Yes   ☐ No

If you answered "No" to any of these questions, you are not alone. Even most real estate agents have not addressed these critical areas—and that's why many families end up fighting over inheritance.

If you answered "Yes" to all three questions, congratulations, you are ahead of most families. However, having a plan is just the beginning. The question becomes: Is your plan optimized to maximize wealth, minimize taxes, and create the outcomes you truly want for your family?

Understand that whether you are starting from scratch or refining an existing strategy, the chapters ahead will show you exactly how to build, protect, and pass on real estate wealth in ways that will bring your family together.

TAKE A MOMENT TO CONSIDER

If your real estate could serve any goal in your life—financial security, family harmony, or legacy building—what would you want it to accomplish? Keep that vision in mind as we explore the framework that makes it possible in the coming chapters.

CHAPTER 2
Your Real Estate Journey Starts With the Right Questions

Twenty years ago, we thought our mission of being successful REALTORS® meant closing deals and making clients happy. We were wrong.

Our perspective changed the day we realized the same painful story kept happening; good families were being blindsided, hurt, and divided. It became clear: This didn't have to happen.

For example, we once worked on a case where a husband passed away while his wife was in memory care, unable to understand what was happening around her. Their daughter had the power of attorney because they obtained it before her mother lost her memory. But the problem was that her brother had been living in the family home and abusing their mother financially, taking her money while she was vulnerable. When their mother needed that money for her care, they were running out of funds. The house had to be sold, but her brother refused to leave. What should have been a time focused on providing the best care for their mother became a legal battle requiring attorneys, a writ of possession, and eventually a half dozen deputies had to physically remove him from the house.

As we reflected on this family's story, we couldn't shake the feeling that their awful experience was not that uncommon. This happens everywhere, to good families, because no one ever teaches them how to plan ahead.

This family's experience led to a question that would define the next two decades of our career: What if we could prevent family disputes instead of just cleaning up the mess after they happen?

If you picked up this book, you're likely experiencing a growing awareness that your real estate situation is more complex than you initially thought. Maybe you are starting to wonder what will happen to your properties when you are gone. Or perhaps you are watching your parents struggle with decisions about their home, or you and your siblings inherited property and do not know what to do with it.

If your mind is full of questions, know that you are not alone, and more importantly, you do not have to stay stuck. There is help.

THE PATTERNS WE DIDN'T RECOGNIZE

Before we discovered a better approach, we watched families hold onto beliefs that felt safe but weren't serving them. We would hear them say, "Someday we will figure it out. The kids will naturally work things out. Putting property in a trust will solve everything."

Through working with these families, we began to recognize the common patterns that kept people stuck, and we started to see where we'd been getting it wrong:

- **We realized many of their decisions were reactive instead of proactive**

Families would call us from hospital beds, saying they needed to sell immediately because they could no longer stay home. Many families lost hundreds of thousands of dollars to capital gains taxes simply because no one had mentioned there were alternatives. Most heartbreaking of all, we would see families destroy relationships over property disputes that could have been prevented with a simple conversation.

- **We assumed people understood their options**

We thought that if someone owned multiple properties, they must know how to measure their performance, understand tax implications, or have a plan for what happens when they're gone. The reality was the opposite—some of our wealthiest clients had the least understanding of what their real estate could do for them. If that's you, it's not your fault. Think about it. Where can we attend classes that help us understand real estate wealth building or tax laws? There's certainly a gap in education and knowledge when it comes to building wealth, protecting wealth, and passing it on. Oftentimes, we'll meet REALTORS ® and financial professionals who know how to buy and sell properties, but not how to help families build, protect, and pass on wealth.

- **We focused on transactions instead of transformations**

The real estate industry taught us that success meant closing deals quickly and efficiently. We'd help someone sell their house and consider the job complete, not realizing that we were missing opportunities to help them understand how their real estate could serve their broader life goals or create strategies that could benefit their family for generations. After three years of traveling and training in over forty cities in America, we've come to understand that there is an education and knowledge gap. It's our mission to close the gap so that more families can prevent family disputes and create generational wealth that matters.

The turning point came when we started understanding what we didn't initially know. Once we started asking different questions outside of real estate, like financial, health, and family dynamics, the new question was, "What do you want your real estate to accomplish for your family?"

THE MOMENT OF CLARITY

After the experience with Hilda, we were on the lookout for more people who felt like they didn't have any options. We wondered, "How could we support our clients with more options outside of only selling their real estate?"

That's when we met Mrs. Arcadia. We spent thirty minutes letting her share memories about everything on her shelf—vivid stories from decades of travel, like standing in line in Istanbul when she bought a little vase, remembering the little girl behind her wearing a beautiful green and turquoise dress. But before that conversation, when we asked what she planned to take from her 2,400 square-foot-house to a 600-square-foot retirement community, she said, "Oh, I'm going to take everything."

Two weeks later, we returned to find everything from that shelf on the floor. When we asked what was happening, she said, "Oh, I'm going to give it away."

That moment taught us that the things in people's homes are valuable to them because of the memories and stories they hold. When she shared those stories with us, she was able to let the physical items go. The value was in her heart and her head, and once she gave us that value through her stories, she was willing to release the items.

It was this experience that changed how we approach families facing transitions. Instead of focusing on what people need to get rid of, we learned to help them honor what matters most to them first.

We learned that asking better questions leads families to realize that they have more options and more control than they ever imagined. They feel empowered to improve their situation.

A NEW APPROACH EMERGES

Today, instead of hoping families will figure things out after a crisis hits, we help them create proactive plans that prevent problems before they start, such as:

- creating simple tools to measure real estate performance, so families know if their real estate is helping them or holding them back,

- mastering strategies for repositioning assets without triggering massive tax consequences, helping families keep more of their wealth while creating better income streams, and

- creating frameworks for family communication that turn potentially explosive inheritance conversations into collaborative planning sessions.

Most importantly, we've learned to help families see their real estate not as buildings, but as wealth waiting to be unlocked which can then be used to pay for health care, prepare for life events, and create options for the future.

So if you are worried about what might happen to everything you have built, you are reading the right book. By the end of these chapters, you will have confidence knowing that you can create a plan that serves your values and takes care of the people you love most.

No matter where you are starting from in your wealth planning journey, we begin with the four pillars of transformation. These pillars represent what becomes possible when real estate shifts from potential family conflict into a tool for generational wealth building and family unity. We're introducing them now so you can see where we're headed and so every chapter between here and there has context.

FOUR PILLARS OF TRANSFORMATION

When families embrace this new approach and actively engage with all four pillars, specific improvements consistently emerge:

1. FINANCIAL CLARITY REPLACES FINANCIAL ANXIETY

Instead of wondering whether your real estate is performing well, you will have concrete data showing exactly how each property contributes to your wealth-building goals. Real Estate Wealth Advisors can help you with an Asset Performance Test to establish this baseline. You will understand your options for optimizing underperforming assets and know the tax implications of every potential decision.

2. FAMILY HARMONY BECOMES THE NORM, NOT THE EXCEPTION

Rather than leaving inheritance decisions to chance, your family will have clear expectations about what everyone will receive and why. Children will understand their future inheritance while you are alive to explain the reasoning and ensure fairness.

3. PROFESSIONAL SUPPORT REPLACES GUESSWORK

Instead of trying to navigate complex real estate and tax strategies alone, you will have a team of specialists who coordinate their efforts to maximize your outcomes. Your Real estate wealth advisor, financial planner, tax consultants, and estate attorney will all be working from the same playbook.

4. PEACE OF MIND BECOMES YOUR DAILY REALITY

Most importantly, you will wake up each morning knowing that your real estate is positioned to serve your life goals, your family has a clear plan for the future, and you are building a legacy that brings people together instead of tearing them apart.

OUR SHARED MISSION

In these pages, what we are working on together is creating a pre-inheritance plan that allows your family to live their biggest life before you are gone.

This work is about understanding your options well enough to make informed decisions and ask the right questions of the right professionals.

The goal of our time together is to help you recognize your real estate as a powerful tool for creating the life and legacy you want. Right now, the most powerful thing you can do to move your family situation forward is surprisingly simple:

Make sure your real estate is in your trust and ask yourself, "When I'm gone, who gets what?"

Checking that your real estate is in your trust and asking, "When I'm gone, who gets what?" will immediately reveal whether you have the clarity and planning that protect families, or whether you are unknowingly setting up the same disputes that tear many families apart.

Do not worry if you discover gaps in your planning. That is why this book exists—to help you identify where you stand today and show you the specific steps to move forward with confidence.

OUR HOPE FOR YOUR JOURNEY

We hope that by learning this question-based approach to real estate wealth planning, you will create a pre-inheritance plan to live your biggest life before you are gone.

Every family that successfully builds, protects, and passes on real estate wealth does the planning while they are alive to see the benefits and ensure everything works the way they intended.

The repair process after someone passes away is challenging at best and impossible at worst. Tax consequences cannot usually be reversed. Family disputes typically get worse over time, and family unrest can go on for generations.

But when you plan ahead, ask the question, "At the end of the day, when I'm gone, do I want my kids to love each other?" and then create a plan to make sure that happens, real estate becomes a tool for strengthening family bonds and creating shared prosperity.

YOUR IDEAL STARTING POINT

This book is specifically designed for baby boomers and their families who own real estate in the United States.

The strategies work especially well for people who own more than one property, but they are valuable for any family that wants to optimize their real estate for maximum benefit.

This book is also for professionals—REALTORS ® , financial planners, trust attorneys, and tax consultants—because right now, it's uncommon to create pre-inheritance plans for real estate. Financial planners typically will not discuss real estate strategies. Estate attorneys usually recommend putting everything in a trust. Tax consultants often advise keeping properties until you pass away.

What is missing for both families and professionals is a proactive approach that integrates all these specialties. Families need guidance that goes beyond traditional advice, and professionals need a framework that helps them collaborate rather than work in silos. Instead of reactive planning that waits for a crisis or death, the solution requires a strategic methodology for using real estate as a tool to build the life that families truly desire while everyone is alive to benefit from and enjoy the results.

FINDING YOUR PLACE IN THIS STORY

If you are reading this and thinking, "This sounds like exactly what our family needs," then you are in the right place. The chapters ahead will walk you through the specific questions to ask, the decisions to consider, and the steps to take based on your unique situation.

If you are thinking, "This sounds interesting, but I'm not sure it applies to us," keep reading. You will be surprised by how many options become available once you start looking at your real estate through the lens of wealth building rather than just property ownership.

And if you are thinking, "This sounds too good to be true," that's understandable. But after twenty years of seeing families transform their situations using these strategies, we can tell you that the approaches are real, available to any family willing to plan ahead, and they work consistently when implemented correctly.

The question is whether you are ready to see your real estate as more than just property and start using it as a tool to create the life and legacy you want.

In the next chapter, we will help you identify the specific obstacles that might be standing between you and the outcomes you want for your family. Because before we can chart the best path forward, we need to understand exactly where you are starting from and what challenges you might be facing.

Let's explore what is ahead for your family's real estate wealth journey.

QUICK ASSESSMENT: IS THIS BOOK FOR YOU?

Take a moment to see if you recognize yourself in any of these situations:

☐ Your home is no longer safe to live in.

☐ You don't know what your options are if you leave your home.

☐ You feel overwhelmed by the thought of having to move

☐ You own real estate but aren't sure if it's performing as well as it could be.

☐ You're concerned about what will happen to your properties when you're gone.

☐ You want to help your children financially but aren't sure how to do it tax-efficiently.

☐ You're wondering if there are better ways to manage your real estate investments.

☐ You've heard about strategies like 1031 exchanges, but don't fully understand how they work.

☐ You want to ensure your family stays together rather than fighting over inheritance.

☐ You're looking for professional guidance but aren't sure what type of advisor you need.

If you checked any of these boxes, the framework ahead will give you the clarity and confidence to move forward with purpose.

YOUR FIRST STRATEGIC QUESTION

Here is a preview of the type of strategic thinking we will explore together. Start with this simple question that will open up entirely different planning possibilities:

Do you own more than one property?

If yes, this means you have investment property beyond your primary residence. This opens up strategies for repositioning assets, creating income streams, and pre-inheritance planning that most people never consider.

If no, you may still have significant opportunities depending on your home's value, your family situation, and your future housing needs.

Either way, this single question can reveal options you might not have known existed. In the chapters ahead, you will discover exactly how to analyze your specific situation and identify the strategies that make the most sense for your family's goals.

CHAPTER 3
The Six Roadblocks

If you ask people over forty, "Have you ever heard of a family fight over real estate after their mom and dad died?" the majority will say yes. They've seen the pain it causes, and for many, it hits close to home.

When the last surviving spouse passes away, real estate usually becomes part of the family's inheritance. Unfortunately, what was once a home often turns into a source of conflict, stress, and financial burden. Most families don't realize that these challenges are preventable. With early planning and open family conversations, sometimes years or even decades in advance, these problems can be avoided. But because many people delay or don't know their options, the burden eventually falls on their loved ones to deal with issues that could have been solved ahead of time.

Through years of helping families navigate real estate challenges, we have identified the six core problems that create the most stress and confusion for real estate owners. The good news is that each of these problems has a solution. Let's walk through them together.

PROBLEM NUMBER 1: THE MOST DANGEROUS PROBLEM OF ALL—"I DON'T SEE A PROBLEM"

The biggest obstacle we encounter is that people do not believe they have a problem in the first place.

We call these the "indifferent property owners," and this is what we see most of. They are living in denial about multiple aspects of their real estate situation, and that denial is costing them and their families dearly. This denial typically shows up in three main areas.

THE HOME DENIAL: "I'M GOING TO DIE IN MY HOUSE"

When it comes to their primary residence, here's what we hear constantly:

- "I'm planning to stay home forever."
- "I'm going to die in my home."
- "My kids will take care of me."
- "I'm still healthy and able-bodied."
- "I'm ninety-five years old, and I don't have a health problem."

The assumption they make is that they are going to remain in the same state of health until the end. They do not realize what the decline feels like, looks like, or that they will inevitably encounter it. They are in denial that they are getting older and going to have problems because, so far, they have not.

They resist facing reality because acknowledging that they are going to have a problem means they will have to change something. Their biggest problem is that they do not want change, but change is going to happen, with or without them.

Many of our clients can see the past clearly, and the present seems okay and doable, but they neglect to consider the future. We ask, "What do you think life will look like in five, ten, or even fifteen years from now? What happens if you can't do the stairs anymore? What happens if you need care?"

As of 2017, only 31% of Americans actually died in their home.[2] Less than a third. Almost everyone says they want to, but they do not. And this same pattern of denial shows up when it comes to their other properties.

THE INVESTMENT PROPERTY DENIAL: "I DON'T NEED THE MONEY"

For their investment properties, the denial sounds different but is equally costly:

- "I don't need the money; I'm not going to be greedy."
- "I'm okay leaving it vacant."
- "I'm okay getting low rent; I like my tenant."
- "It's in a trust, so it's safe."

Many families look at their property and see only a building, not the wealth, security, and options it could create for the people they love. When they don't recognize its true power, they unintentionally overlook opportunities that could change their family's lives for generations.

For instance, we met a man who was receiving $700 rent on a property worth $2,800 in market rent because he had a great, long-time tenant living there. He had a mortgage on the property, so he was actually losing money every month. When we asked him, "Do you think you're stewarding your wealth well?" he replied, "No, I guess I'm not stewarding my wealth very well." He decided to sell his property, utilizing a 1031 exchange deferring capital gain tax, and buying a leveraged DST with higher income. The non-recourse loan in the DST replaced his mortgage. In the end, he was making more money, and he did not have a mortgage. He had been in denial about his situation, and this kind of denial runs even deeper when it comes to estate planning.

THE ESTATE PLANNING DENIAL: "MY KIDS WILL SHARE IT"

Even families who believe they've planned are often one misunderstanding away from disaster. We met a man who owned three properties and didn't even know trusts existed. He had no clue that, without one, everything he'd built would be dragged through probate—leaving his loved ones to deal with the mess.

Others have trusts, but they are inadequate. Most trusts simply say, "My kids will share it." But, how do you share real estate? You don't. You fight over it.

Even when the trust says to "sell it and divide it," it typically does not say when. So one sibling can say, "I don't want to sell it now," while another may say, "I want my money now." That is where family wars begin. The good news is that these problems are not insurmountable, but they do require the right approach.

In any of these cases of denial, the key is to help them discover their problem themselves through the right questions.

THE HOME DENIAL: "I'M GOING TO DIE IN MY HOUSE"

- "Should we be blessed to live long enough, can we agree that we're all going to need some level of help?"

- "Do you think it's easier to downsize now, or downsize in ten years from now?"

- "Will you be younger or older then? Will it be harder or easier?"

THE INVESTMENT PROPERTY DENIAL: "I DON'T NEED THE MONEY"

- "Do you believe money is good for the good it does?"

- "Do you believe that real estate is money— we just haven't turned it into money?"

- "Is it your job, as a trustee, to steward this wealth as best as you can for the benefit of your loved ones?"

- "You have two choices with investment property: You can be a true investor, or you can be a philanthropist. Which do you want to be?"

This is when people finally realize, "Actually, I have a problem that I didn't know I had."

What it comes down to is that if you do not think you have a problem, that *is* the problem. Because while you are sitting in denial, opportunities are being missed, wealth is being wasted, and your family's future is being put at risk.

The first step to solving any problem is recognizing it exists, and the clock is ticking, whether you acknowledge it or not. While recognizing the problem is important, the deeper question touches on something more fundamental about how you view your role with the wealth you've been given:

ARE YOU BEING A GOOD STEWARD OF WHAT YOU'VE BUILT?

Even when families have all the legal documents in place, there's a deeper question that rarely gets asked.

"Do you believe you're the best steward of the wealth you've created?"

When we ask this, people often pause. They've never thought about their properties this way because they see themselves as owners, not stewards. But there's a difference between the two.

As Christians, we believe most people would choose to be a good steward with the wealth they've created. Deep down, they want to be wise stewards because they care about what they've built and the legacy they'll leave behind. But the truth is, many are unsure, overwhelmed, or simply indifferent because no one has ever shown them how to steward that wealth with intention.

And that quiet indifference is what puts families at risk.

In the Bible, Jesus tells a story about a leader who entrusts three individuals with different amounts of resources before leaving on a long trip (Matthew 25:14-30, NIV). Two of them invest and multiply what they were given, while the third hides his portion out of fear and does nothing with it. When the leader returns, he celebrates the ones who used their gifts wisely and challenges the one who held back.

This story reminds us that everything we have, our time, abilities, finances, and opportunities, is entrusted to us. We're called to be good stewards, to use what we've been given with intention and courage, and to grow it in a way that honors God.

When we meet with families who have multiple properties sitting vacant or underperforming, we gently ask, "Is this good stewardship? Is this wealth working for the good it could do?"

Most realize they've been like that third servant, not out of malice or greed, but out of uncertainty. They're holding onto properties because they don't know what else to do. They're afraid of making the wrong decision, so they make no decision at all.

Stewardship is intentional. You can ask yourself:

- "Is this property serving its highest purpose?"
- "Could this wealth be doing more good—for my family, for others, for the Kingdom?"

- "Am I multiplying what's been entrusted to me, or am I hiding it out of fear?"

The families who embrace this stewardship mindset are the ones who find peace with their decisions. They stop seeing themselves as stuck with properties and start seeing themselves as entrusted with opportunities.

Our goal is to help you become the best steward possible and honor God by doing so. Because at the end of the day, good stewardship means you manage your properties with purpose, intention, and wisdom that creates blessings for generations to come.

You might want to be a good steward and might even feel called to do something different with your properties, but when you start thinking about what to actually do, the uncertainty becomes overwhelming. Which brings us to the second major obstacle families face.

PROBLEM NUMBER 2: THE OPTIONS OVERWHELM—"I DON'T KNOW WHAT TO DO WITH MY REAL ESTATE"

Being paralyzed by options is the most common obstacle we encounter. Property owners, whether they have inherited real estate, own investment properties, or are aging in their primary residence, often feel overwhelmed by the choices in front of them. They know something needs to change, but they are locked in uncertainty.

Maybe their home no longer works for them, but they don't know what alternatives exist. It could be that they have inherited a property and are not sure whether to sell, rent, or keep it. Or they might own investment properties that feel more like burdens than assets, but they cannot envision a different path forward.

When you feel overwhelmed, the natural response is to do nothing. Uncertainty leads to inaction, which is why so many homes across America sit vacant while families try to figure out what to do. We are talking about millions of dollars of real estate sitting empty, deteriorating, and creating ongoing expenses, all because owners simply don't know what steps to take next.

The key to breaking through this paralysis is information, specifically, the *right* information about your unique situation and goals. The solution starts with discovery, both self-discovery and discovering the true wealth potential of your properties. Through a series of targeted questions, we help you uncover what you really want and need from your real estate.

Rather than overwhelming you with a hundred options at once, we take a surgical approach to problem-solving. Think of this process like a surgeon who makes precise cuts to address specific issues. We use questions to isolate each challenge and address it one by one. This converts an overwhelming decision into a series of manageable choices.

We also connect you with a real estate wealth advisor who can show you options you may never have considered, including 1031 exchanges that eliminate capital gains taxes and repositioning strategies that turn properties into passive income streams.

PROBLEM NUMBER 3: THE COGNITIVE BURDEN— "MY PROPERTIES ARE CONSTANTLY ON MY MIND"

Even when property owners begin to understand their options, they often discover that the true challenge is the constant mental weight these properties create. Property ownership creates what we call a "cognitive burden"—the mental and emotional weight of constantly worrying about your real estate. This burden affects both property owners and their families.

For property owners, the cognitive burden includes:

- worrying about the "terrible T's": tenants, toilets, termites, trash, and taxes,

- rising insurance costs and property taxes that reduce cash flow,

- concerns about family disputes: "I know my kids can't handle this when I'm gone," or "I know my kids are going to fight,"

- fear about maintenance issues and aging infrastructure, and

- Stress about making the "right" decisions about when to sell, hold, or renovate.

For family members, the cognitive burden looks different but is equally real:

- adult children who quit their jobs to care for aging parents,

- spouses worried about their ability to provide care: "I promised to take care of this person for the rest of my life, and I don't know if I can,"

- the emotional weight of potentially placing a loved one in a care facility.

Then, there are siblings with different financial needs that create family tension. We address cognitive burden through three key approaches.

First, we facilitate family conversations that prevent conflicts before they start. Rather than letting family members discover each other's different needs and timelines during a crisis, we help families communicate openly while everyone is healthy and able to participate in decision-making.

Second, we help create pre-inheritance plans that eliminate uncertainty. Through strategies like 1031 exchanges, we can help you sell one property and buy three—allowing you to bless your children fairly while you're alive to see the benefit. This removes the guesswork and potential disputes with proper pre-inheritance planning.

Third, we provide practical solutions for the day-to-day burdens. When property taxes rise, insurance costs increase, or tenants complain, you'll have a clear framework for making decisions rather than feeling trapped by circumstances. Our approach reduces stress by providing clarity, options, and a clear path forward.

PROBLEM NUMBER 4: THE PHYSICAL BURDEN— "OUR PROPERTY IS FALLING APART"

While the mental burden of property ownership can weigh heavily on your mind, there is often a very real, physical side to the stress as well. The physical burden represents the tangible, structural challenges that make properties feel overwhelming rather than valuable.

These problems include:

- deferred maintenance that has gotten out of hand,

- vacant properties that neighbors are complaining about,

- properties that can't be rented because of broken HVAC systems, leaking roofs, or other major issues,

- homes that can't be insured due to structural problems,

- properties that are no longer safe to live in, and

- homes that won't support aging in place.

The physical burden often feeds into the cognitive burden. Every time you see that broken railing or receive a complaint from neighbors, it adds to your mental stress. For many property owners, the physical deterioration feels insurmountable, leading them to simply avoid dealing with the property altogether.

Rather than letting physical problems overwhelm you or force you into costly decisions, we start with clarity about what makes financial sense. Before diving into repairs, we help you answer the crucial question: "Is it worth fixing?"

The physical condition of the property often impacts the financial side. Properties with deferred maintenance typically cannot generate as much income. Through asset performance testing and property repair analysis, we determine whether investing in repairs makes economic sense or whether you'd be better served by selling as-is.

To determine if repairs make sense, we start by putting a value on selling the property as is. Then we show you an after-repair value (ARV), along with the accurate and current repair costs, to validate if it makes sense. This is where we train Real Estate Wealth Advisors to help you fix up your homes. We also have an entire construction team, an interior designer, and anybody you need so that it can be sold for the most amount of money. Most real estate agents do not offer this level of support, but we train Real Estate Wealth Advisors to have solutions that solve the problems that get in people's way.

Furthermore, we help you understand how physical improvements align with your long-term goals, whether that is maximizing sale price, improving rental income, or preparing a property for family use. Sometimes the best solution is not fixing the property at all. Through 1031 exchanges, you can sell a property with deferred maintenance and buy something newer, smaller, or in a different location: a property that produces the cash flow you need without the ongoing headaches.

PROBLEM NUMBER 5: THE FINANCIAL CHALLENGE—"I WANT TO SELL BUT..."

Beyond the physical deterioration and ongoing maintenance headaches, there is often an even deeper concern that troubles property owners: money. Many property owners feel trapped by financial considerations they do not fully understand.

The most common concerns include:

- "I want to sell, but I don't want to pay capital gains taxes."

- "I'm scared I'll run out of money if I make the wrong decision."

- "I want to make more money from my properties, but I don't know how."

- "I don't understand the tax consequences of my options."

- "I need to pay for health care."

These financial fears often prevent property owners from taking any action at all, even when their current situation is not serving them well.

They end up holding onto underperforming assets because they're afraid of making a costly mistake.

The antidote to financial fear is knowledge. Specifically, understanding what options are actually available to you. We start by helping you see your real estate as an asset worth money, not just a house with doors and windows that somebody lives in.

Let's say you bought a property for $1 million that's now worth $2 million, but you like your tenant and haven't increased your rent to market rate. This means your property is underperforming. Through asset performance testing, we measure your property like you would a stock or bond. If that $2 million property is only making a 1% rate of return, but you could sell it through a 1031 exchange and buy into something generating 5%, you've just increased your income significantly.

For those who are tired of management, tenants, and all the problems that come with rental properties, the 1031 exchange is not the only answer. You see, the 1031 exchange requires you to sell a rental property and buy another rental property, which does not remove the tenant and management problems. Many of our clients, when asked the question "Would you prefer an active or passive investment?" they pick passive.

One route to selling an investment property and buying a *true* investment property with no headaches is the Delaware Statutory Trusts (DST). Through a 1031 exchange into a DST, capital gains tax will be deferred, and your property becomes professionally managed. It feels like an annuity, where you receive money every month without having to worry about anything. You will never receive a phone call from a tenant, and you will not have to repair a dishwasher or garbage disposal.

In our experience, DSTs generally provide around 5% net return, which is often better than properties in most high-land-value areas. There are DSTs that deliver a higher rate of return but also with higher risk. Most of our clients are older and prefer the asset preservation route and end up a bit more conservative than a younger investor.

What we have learned through years of experience is that capital gains taxes are the number one enemy to generational wealth, but most people don't know much about them or how to plan for them. Our approach focuses on education first, then implementation of the right strategy for your specific situation.

PROBLEM NUMBER 6: THE URGENCY GAP— "THERE'S NO RUSH…UNTIL THERE IS"

While financial fears paralyze some property owners, there is an equally problematic opposite reaction: a complete lack of concern. And that lack of urgency can be just as costly. When families inherit real estate worth millions of dollars, those who are financially stable often feel no pressure to make decisions. They can afford to let properties sit vacant or underperform because they do not need the income immediately.

But when one family member needs money urgently, they are pitted against siblings who are not in a rush. Suddenly, what should be a family blessing becomes a source of conflict and legal disputes.

This urgency gap is especially dangerous for aging homeowners who put off key decisions. Once health declines, and choices aren't made in time, "I'll deal with it later" turns into emergency decision-making for loved ones, leaving families stressed, unprepared, and forced to make rushed decisions they never wanted to make.

The solution to both urgency imbalance and procrastination is creating a plan while everyone is still on the same page. We help families address potential conflicts before they become urgent by focusing on communication and clear documentation.

We help families create comprehensive pre-inheritance plans that go beyond simply having a trust that says "three kids share it." Trusts protect the family from the property having to go through probate, but do not prevent family disputes. Our plans include specific instructions about timing, decision-making processes, and what to do if family members disagree.

We also help families understand that "keeping it for the kids" is not always what the kids actually want. As we often discover, children do not want the property itself—they want the value within it. Having these conversations while parents are alive prevents the common scenario where "one of the kids wants to keep it, and the other two want to sell it" after parents pass away.

For aging property owners, we emphasize the importance of proactive rather than reactive planning. We often ask families, "At the end of the day, when you're gone, do you want your kids to love each other? What's your plan to make sure that happens?"

The reality is that most families have not thought through these questions yet. This is normal, and it is also exactly why taking the time to understand your current situation is so valuable. Working through the decision tree below will help you identify your priority path and focus your energy where it matters most.

SELF-ASSESSMENT: WHERE DO YOU STAND?

The key to moving forward is understanding your current situation through the right questions. This decision tree will help you determine your next steps:

Start Here

Do you need income from your investment properties to sustain the life you desire?

If YES → Your priority is maximizing performance:

- If you could make more money from your properties, would you?

- Your path focuses on asset performance testing and optimization strategies

If NO → Your priority may be legacy planning:

- If you could bless your family while you're alive, would you?

- Your path focuses on pre-inheritance planning and wealth repositioning

ADDITIONAL QUESTIONS TO CONSIDER

- Are you keeping properties "for the kids"—but have you asked them if they want that specific property or the value of the property itself?

- What's your plan for when you can't stay home anymore?

- Do you know how to avoid the tax consequences of your real estate decisions?

- Do you believe you will run out of money? What is your plan?

NEXT STEPS

Based on your answers, you will know whether to focus on income optimization, family legacy planning, or addressing immediate concerns about your living situation. The following chapters will give you the specific strategies for whichever path applies to your situation.

MOVING FORWARD TOGETHER

Whether your decision tree led you toward income optimization, legacy planning, or addressing immediate housing concerns, these are common paths that countless families have navigated successfully. Nearly every real estate owner faces some combination of these challenges. The important thing to understand is that each path has proven solutions, and you do not have to figure it out by yourself.

In the next chapter, we will explore the shift from reactive to proactive planning and help you understand when and how to work with a real estate wealth advisor who can guide you through your options.

The goal is to turn overwhelming problems into manageable decisions and burdensome assets into wealth-building tools that serve your family for generations to come.

CHAPTER 4

How to Get Your Family on the Same Page

A few years ago, a woman approached us at a seniors' event. She said, "I need help. I need to sell my mom's house in two years, but my brother wants to sell it now, and he is difficult to work with."

Sensing the urgency in her voice, we sat down to listen to her side of the story. During our conversation, the woman seemed so sweet and appeared to be in an impossible situation.

Then we met with the woman's brother, and after hearing his side of the story, we realized things were not as they seemed.

He was a level-headed person. As the trustee, he felt responsible for looking out for all parties, and the majority wanted to sell right then. His sister wanted to wait two years; he believed they needed to act sooner. They simply weren't seeing eye to eye.

After many conversations with all three siblings, they decided to sell the family home and split the funds. We helped them declutter and repair both structures on the property. In the end, each sibling used their share differently: the sister purchased a place of her own to live in, one brother helped his son purchase his first home, and the other brother helped his daughter with her business.

What started as a phone call filled with frustration became a story of three siblings building on their parents' legacy in their own ways.

This situation shows that when emotions run high and everyone believes they are right, it becomes difficult for everyone to move forward. So, how do you find solutions when each person sees the situation completely differently?

One trick we've learned is to ask people what they want to do, instead of telling them what they should do. This works even for families who are stuck and have relationships hanging by a thread.

This shift highlights our secret key as Real Estate Wealth Advisors. It's what makes our entire business work. Without it, clients would stay overwhelmed and paralyzed. We're talking about one simple but powerful tool: questions.

HOW WE LEARNED QUESTIONS WORK BETTER THAN ADVICE

Years ago, we noticed a pattern: The families who made progress were the ones who discovered their own answers.

After that observation, we started studying our strategy sessions more closely. What was leading these families to draw conclusions on their own? One thing stood out: the number of questions asked. In one hour, we asked anywhere from sixty to eighty questions!

These sessions and the wonderful families who went through them taught us that families move forward on difficult property decisions when they don't feel sold or pushed into something. Instead, they feel like they're making their own decisions because they truly are. Proper questions help them self-discover that they need to see the world just a little differently. No one wants to be told what to do.

Here's what we learned about the difference between giving advice and asking questions:

THE TRADITIONAL ADVICE APPROACH (WHAT SOME PROFESSIONALS DO)

- Tell families what they should do based on standard practices,

- presents solutions before fully understanding individual circumstances,

- creates resistance because families feel pushed into decisions, and

- often leads to inaction because family members don't feel ownership of the solution.

THE QUESTION-BASED APPROACH (OUR METHOD):

- guides families to discover their own answers through strategic questions,

- understands and adapts to each family's unique dynamics and priorities,

- generates buy-in because families reach their own conclusions, and

- creates momentum because people naturally act on decisions they make themselves.

Take the story we shared earlier about the woman and her brother. If we had used the traditional approach, we might have immediately advised like: "You need to communicate better with your brother," or "Here's what most families do in trust disputes" Instead, we asked questions of both siblings separately:

- "Help me understand what you're hoping to accomplish here."

- "What's most important to you about honoring your parents' wishes?"

- "What would need to happen for you to feel good about this outcome?"

Through these questions, we discovered the brother was actually the most level-headed family member, and was simply trying to fulfill his duty as trustee according to his parents' written instructions. The sister felt overwhelmed and was projecting her frustration onto him. By asking instead of assuming, we helped them both see the situation clearly and work together rather than against each other.

Every family has its own story. That is why our approach starts with questions that honor your specific situation. If you own multiple properties, we focus there. If your greatest concern is protecting the family home, that is where we begin. Our framework is built to meet you where you are, so you feel understood, supported, and confident about the legacy you will leave.

For investment properties, we start with questions that can look like:

- "Do you need the income from your investment property to sustain the life you desire?"

- "If you could make more money, would you?"

- "If you could bless your family while you're alive, would you?"

For families, we ask about their specific dynamics, such as: "Are all your kids alike? Do they think alike? Do they act alike? Are they in the same economic phase of life?"

When the answer is no to all of these, and it almost always is, we gently explain a hard truth: The data says that 70% of families end up fighting.[4] Not because they don't love each other, but because they're at different stages of life, with various pressures, priorities, and expectations.

And when real money, more than any of them has ever handled before, is suddenly on the table, those differences turn into conflict.

The question-based approach works here because it helps families see the reality of their situation before it becomes a crisis. Instead of assuming everyone will get along, the questions reveal where

---

4 Roy Williams and Vic Preisser. *Preparing Heirs: Five Steps to a Successful Transition of Family Wealth and Values*. Robert D. Reed Publishers, 2003.

potential conflicts might arise. More importantly, these questions open up conversations about solutions while everyone is still healthy and able to participate in planning.

In the next few sections, we'll dive into five of the most common concerns that families have when they come to work with us. We hope that by addressing them here, we'll help you feel prepared to take the next step and set your family up for success.

QUESTION 1: "WHAT IF I DON'T KNOW THE ANSWERS TO THESE QUESTIONS?"

Exposing things that you don't know the answer to is the point of our time together. These questions aren't meant to have right or wrong answers, but to help you figure out what matters most to you. When someone says, "I don't know," that tells us exactly where to focus next.

Many people, when we ask them a question, do not actually answer it. They go sideways on us. We will ask a specific question, and they will start talking about something else entirely. When that happens, we stop and say, "Let me ask the question again."

When the conversation gets uncomfortable, people naturally try to avoid it. They shift topics, give half-answers, or say they "might" know. But avoidance is what puts families at risk. The truth is, honest answers, especially "I don't know," are the key to creating solutions that prevent conflict and protect the people they care about. Courage in these moments is what saves families from heartache later.

The power of this approach lies in creating a safe space for uncertainty. When families feel they can admit what they don't know without judgment, they become open to discovering new possibilities. This honesty about gaps in their knowledge or planning becomes the foundation for finding practical solutions.

After experiencing this type of conversation, many families wonder how this differs from traditional professional advice.

QUESTION 2: "HOW IS A QUESTION-BASED APPROACH DIFFERENT FROM JUST GETTING ADVICE FROM A FINANCIAL PLANNER OR ATTORNEY?"

Most professionals start by telling you what they think you should do based on their area of specialty. We start by helping you discover what you truly want to do—what matters most to your family and your future. With that clarity, you can walk into any attorney's, CPA's, or advisor's office and know exactly what to ask for, making their work more effective and your decisions more meaningful.

For the wealthy, real estate consistently makes up about a quarter to a third of their portfolios. For Baby Boomers in particular, it is often their largest single asset, sometimes representing half or more of their net worth.[5] They have a financial planner, a trust attorney, and a CPA. But most do not have a real estate plan. We spoke with a man with around

---

5 Williams, Roy, and Vic Preisser. *Preparing Heirs: Five Steps to a Successful Transition of Family Wealth and Values.* Robert D. Reed Publishers, 2003.

thirty million dollars in real estate assets, and when we asked him who plans his real estate, he said, "I guess I do. But I don't do anything because I don't plan it."

Most property owners don't know how to measure their real estate, its value, or what they could do with it. The biggest problem we see is in their mindset. Most people see their property as a house with doors, windows, and a roof. We see it as an asset that, when unlocked, can provide increased income, create true passive income, or even bless a loved one.

Think about it this way: When you have a health concern, you go to a doctor. For financial matters, you turn to a financial planner. For taxes, you seek out a CPA, but when it comes to real estate—the largest asset most families own—most people say, "I'll figure it out, I'll keep it till I die, or ask a Realtor." The challenge is that most REALTORS ® focus only on buying and selling because that is how they make money. They are not trained to analyze wealth or design strategies that protect and grow it, nor do they understand how to unlock wealth and reposition it to what matters most to the owner.

Financial planners, CPAs, and trust attorneys often do not know how to do 1031 exchanges or what the options are for real estate. They just know it is real estate, and you keep it until you die. They do not realize there are other routes.

On the other hand, a real estate wealth advisor helps you build, protect, and pass on wealth. We are like shepherds who guide you down the path that you want to go, providing expertise and resources once you are clear on your direction.

This approach addresses the gap that exists in most people's professional teams. While they have financial planners, CPAs, and attorneys, they lack someone who specializes in real estate wealth strategies. The question-based approach ensures you get the right guidance for your specific situation rather than generic advice that may not fit your family's goals.

Of course, this leads to another concern many families have.

QUESTION 3: "WILL THIS WORK IF MY FAMILY DOESN'T GET ALONG?"

The moments when families do not see eye to eye are exactly when the right questions matter most. Arguments usually happen because everyone is talking, but no one is truly listening. Good questions shift that dynamic. They move the conversation away from defending positions and toward exploring options together so families can find common ground.

Family chaos often begins when there is judgment instead of curiosity. Some siblings have more time than money, while others have more money than time, and that is where disputes arise. The right questions change everything. Asking, "Who do you turn to in your family?" or "Are your kids in the same stage of life?" uncovers the real dynamics before they turn into problems.

When adult children are forced to make decisions about valuable assets that are not theirs, conflict is almost inevitable. Old childhood wounds resurface once parents are gone, and emotions take over. By asking the right questions while everyone is healthy and thinking clearly, families can address these dynamics early and prevent the chaos that comes with reactive planning.

While understanding the family dynamics is crucial, many people also want to know about the practical aspects of this process.

QUESTION 4: "HOW LONG DOES THIS PROCESS TAKE?"

While the questioning process is ongoing and does not end after one conversation, most families start seeing clarity within the first strategy session. The turning point happens when they stop feeling stuck and start seeing possibilities they didn't know existed. We believe that knowledge is what we know today, but imagination is what could be in the future. We cannot change the past, only the future.

That's why we conduct comprehensive hour-long strategy sessions where we typically ask sixty to eighty questions. The exact number varies depending on each family's pace. Some people process decisions quickly, while others prefer to carefully consider each question before responding.

Our approach is never one-size-fits-all. Every family's journey looks different because what matters most to you determines the path we take. For some, the priority is creating immediate income. For others, it is building and protecting a long-term legacy. The solutions are always tailored to your family's unique goals and circumstances.

The process works because we come from curiosity, not judgment. When people are not moving forward, instead of saying, "It's been six months, and you haven't done anything," we ask, "What's getting in your way?" We let them be the judge of their own situation, knowing that we are the stewards helping them build wealth.

Once they start answering the right questions, they realize they have options they never knew existed. That is when the timeline speeds up dramatically.

Beyond timing considerations, there is another aspect of this process that concerns many people.

QUESTION 5: "WHAT IF THE QUESTIONS BRING UP DIFFICULT TOPICS?"

The questions we ask during a session may bring up difficult topics, but avoiding those topics does not make them disappear; it just makes them harder to deal with later. The families who address these topics early are the ones who stay close.

Most families avoid the hard conversations, believing everything will work out. But when parents hold onto beliefs like, "I'm never leaving my house," their children are often left to deal with chaos and conflict. We have seen the heartbreak—families torn apart because they waited too long, even a brother on his deathbed whose final wish was simply for his siblings to get along.

Questions provide a framework for having these difficult conversations while emotions are not running high, and everyone can participate. Having an experienced, unbiased guide to facilitate these discussions makes all the difference. Family members feel safer opening up when there is someone who understands the complexities but cares about the family's well-being without favoring any particular family member. Instead of leaving families to figure things out during a crisis, the questioning process creates space for honest discussions about fears, expectations, and plans when everyone is still capable of making thoughtful decisions.

Of course, all of this information may raise a final question: Does this approach actually work in practice?

THE EVIDENCE IS IN THE OUTCOMES

The statistics on family disputes over real estate tell the story. Attorneys claim that there is a 70% failure rate on wealth transfers, which is often attributed largely to family dynamics.[6] But look at the families

---

6 Williams, Roy, and Vic Preisser. *Preparing Heirs: Five Steps to a Successful Transition of Family Wealth and Values.* Robert D. Reed Publishers, 2003.

who plan ahead and have these conversations early. That number drops dramatically.

We have seen this statistic proven over and over. Families who thought they were stuck and assumed their only option was to keep properties they did not want, or sell properties they could not afford to sell. Once they started asking the right questions, they discovered options they never knew existed.

Take the 1031 exchange. Most property owners have heard of it, but they do not know if it makes sense for their situation. Instead of explaining the technical details, we ask, "If you could move your wealth from this property to something that better fits your goals, what would that look like?" That one question opens up possibilities they had not considered.

Or consider family dynamics. Instead of assuming we know what each family member wants, we ask them individually, "What would need to happen for you to feel good about this decision?" The answers often surprise everyone, including the person answering.

The question-based approach works because it honors something most people overlook. Families want to make good decisions; they just need help discovering what "good" means for their specific situation.

Real Estate Wealth Advisors who use this approach see different results than those who do not. Their clients make decisions they feel confident about years later, rather than only focusing on completing transactions. On the other hand, their families create legacies that strengthen family bonds for generations while passing on wealth.

The evidence of this strengthening is in the outcomes. Families who go through this process report less stress, better relationships, and more confidence in their financial future because they discovered what they wanted to do.

That is the power of the right questions at the right time. This is why we have shared our question-based approach with you, because getting your family on the same page means asking the right questions that help each family member discover what matters most to them, and then building a plan around those shared discoveries.

Now it is time to experience the power of questions for yourself.

DISCOVER YOUR PATH: THE RIGHT QUESTIONS FOR YOUR FAMILY

Now that you understand the power of questions, it is time to start asking yourself the right ones. This assessment will help you determine your current situation and next steps.

First, the foundational question for your home:

Would you like to make the decision of where and when your next move will be, or would you like to leave it up to somebody else?

This is the difference between being proactive and reactive. The proactive person says, "I want to decide where and when I'll go—so I'm going to start planning now." The reactive person says, "I'll just stay here until something happens, and let someone else figure it out."

If you choose to make your own decisions, then ask yourself: Do you have a plan for when you can't stay home?

Next, the essential question for parents:

At the end of the day, when you're gone, is your goal that your kids love each other?

If your answer is yes, then the follow-up question is: What's your plan to make sure that happens?

For your investment properties:

Do you need the income from your investment properties to sustain the life you desire?

If YES: Your next question is: "If you could make more money from your properties, would you?" Your path focuses on optimizing asset performance, which really means more income.

If NO: Your next question is: "If you could bless your family while you're alive, would you?" Your path focuses on pre-inheritance planning and wealth repositioning that is designed to bless your loved ones.

Key reflection questions:

- How's your current plan working?

- Are you answering these questions honestly, or are you avoiding things that scare you?

- What's getting in your way if you're not moving forward?

One of the keys to success is answering questions honestly and not avoiding things that scare you. The vast majority of people say, "I'm not going to have a problem," but if that's true, why do many families have disputes?

Based on your answers, you now know whether you need to focus on proactive planning for your home, optimizing your investment properties, or creating a plan to keep your family together. The following chapters will give you the specific strategies for your path.

CHAPTER 5

Why Good Intentions Are Not Enough

Did you know that children ask around 40,000 questions between the ages of two and five?[7]

Think back to when you were that age…your instinct was pure curiosity! You were not trying to sell anyone anything or prove how smart you were. All you wanted was to understand the world around you.

But somewhere along the way, we all got reprogrammed. We learned that asking too many questions may annoy people. Teachers told us we should already know the answers. Society

---

7 Warren Berger, *A More Beautiful Question: The Power of Inquiry to Spark Breakthrough Ideas* (New York: Bloomsbury USA, 2014), 38.

convinced us that telling people what to do was more valuable than helping them discover what they need.

This programming creates a fundamental problem that affects everyone involved in real estate wealth planning, and it is probably why previous attempts to solve your real estate challenges have not worked.

The catch is not with real estate itself, but with how most people approach real estate planning. Let's look at what is really happening.

THE PROBLEM MOST PEOPLE DON'T SEE

Most people believe they can manage their real estate on their own. They assume they will stay healthy, remain in their home forever, and that everything will somehow work out for their family after they are gone.

This unrealistic belief leads to a breakdown in planning. People think they are being responsible by owning real estate, but they are actually creating problems by not having a plan for what happens next.

The same pattern shows up everywhere: Everyone thinks they are handling their real estate properly, but most of the time, they are making decisions based on assumptions rather than actual analysis.

The difference is critical. An assumption-based decision ignores real data, performance, costs, and consequences, while an informed decision is grounded in clarity about what you have and the options available. Most people operate on assumptions, and that is when problems they never saw coming appear.

For example, they assume their three adult children will somehow figure out how to share a rental property, not realizing that real estate cannot be split like a bank account. Or they think keeping the family home "for the kids" is a gift, without asking if their children actually want a house built in 1952 or if they would prefer the money to buy something that fits their own lifestyle.

We see this constantly. Parents will say, "My daughter wants the property," but when we ask how that works with the other two children, they have not thought it through. Maybe they will give her a discount, and she will buy out the siblings, but then how do the other children receive that same value? They do not think about how this looks to the family when they are gone. The siblings will assume the daughter who received the benefit did something to earn special treatment, creating resentment that could last generations. These conflicts are predictable and preventable, but only when families understand the dynamics before they create permanent plans.

This kind of assumption-based thinking shows up in how people approach their entire real estate situation. Think about the difference between these two approaches:

TRADITIONAL APPROACH

- "I'll keep the properties for the kids."
- "My trust will handle everything."
- "I'll deal with it when the time comes."

REAL ESTATE WEALTH ADVISOR APPROACH

- "Have you asked your kids if they actually want the properties?"

- "Do you know how much care will cost when you need it?"

- "What happens if you can't divide a property three ways?"

The contrast between these approaches is striking. The first set of statements assumes everything will work out, while the second set focuses on understanding the real challenges before they become crises.

Most people have been conditioned to think that owning real estate is automatically good planning. So when someone suggests they need to manage their real estate wealth actively, their first instinct is to resist.

But what does that resistance look like in practice?

- "I'm fine where I am."

- "The kids will figure it out."

- "My trust takes care of everything."

The planning stops before it even begins.

This breakdown in planning hurts everyone involved. Families get frustrated because they inherit complicated situations they do not know how to handle. Property owners stay stuck because they think planning means giving up control. But how exactly did this avoidance take hold, and why does it affect so many families?

THE AVOIDANCE PROBLEM

Avoidance of proper planning affects people in specific ways, creating barriers that keep families from getting the help they actually need.

Property owners stop asking important questions because they think planning means facing uncomfortable realities about aging, health, and mortality. They worry that talking about "what happens if" scenarios will make them more likely to happen.

On the other hand, many family members stay silent about real estate planning because they are afraid it will seem like they only care about the inheritance. So they wait, hoping their parents will bring it up first.

This avoidance is completely understandable given our cultural conditioning around these topics. Most people have never been taught how to have these conversations, and there are few good models for how families can discuss wealth planning without creating tension.

This results in two generations of people who could help each other plan for the future, but they are both stuck avoiding the conversation.

And unfortunately, even when people *do* understand the importance of planning ahead, there is still a catch. People can create plans based on incomplete information.

WHEN PLANNING BACKFIRES

Planning done poorly can be just as harmful as not planning at all. We've had clients tell us their investment properties are "doing great" even though they haven't raised the rent in fifteen years. Families insist they have everything handled because they have a trust, not realizing the trust doesn't explain how to divide a property that can't be split. Others say they're "not worried about becoming a burden" without any idea what care actually costs.

The challenge with this mindset is that property owners are making decisions with limited information. Admitting a rental might be underperforming means facing the possibility that money has been left on the table for years. And realizing a trust may not prevent family disputes means confronting the hard truth that good intentions alone are not enough to protect family relationships.

When someone acknowledges that their current plan might have gaps, they are confronting years of decisions they thought were solid. Not only are these real estate problems, but they are challenges to everything they thought they knew about taking care of their family.

That is why surface-level planning and accepting simple answers will not work. People need time and space to work through the true complexity of their situation. Sometimes it takes seeing numbers before they understand their property's performance, while other times it takes calculating care costs before they grasp the financial reality.

For example, instead of accepting "my trust handles everything," we might show them what happens when three adult children inherit a property together but cannot agree on whether to sell, rent, or move in. Each scenario reveals another layer of the real situation until we get to what is at stake beneath the surface.

This point in the process is where patience becomes critical. The goal is to help them see all the factors they might not have considered so they can make truly informed decisions.

THE MISSING ANALYSIS

Thinking proactively is the first step, but clarity without data only gets you so far. The piece that makes action possible is honest measurement of where you stand. Once a property owner understands the avoidance problem, they can see why so many families end up in disputes. And when people start asking the right questions, they finally begin to see their real situation clearly. With all these pieces in place, it might seem like the path forward is clear.

But wanting to do the right thing is not enough when you are dealing with complex real estate situations.

You may want to take care of your family and avoid being a burden, but if you do not have data about your properties and costs for your future, nothing changes. We have seen too many families spend months discussing "doing something" about their real estate situation, only to realize they do not know where to start because they do not have the basic information they need to make decisions.

One may think this is considered poor planning, but in reality, people are trying to make important decisions without the right tools. We believe people do the best they can with the knowledge they have. The problem is that there is not enough training focused on making these decisions.

Real estate wealth planning only works when it is connected to analysis and concrete options. When someone realizes, through questions, that keeping multiple rental properties might burden their children, the next step is data. They need to see the numbers: cash flow, appreciation rates, management costs, and tax implications.

Similarly, when they discover that they might not be able to stay in their home long-term, they need information about care costs, senior living options, and what transitioning looks like financially and logistically. But having the right analysis is only part of what makes real estate wealth planning truly effective.

THE INFORMATION-BASED APPROACH

Instead of making assumptions about what is best for your family, we have learned to help you gather the information you need to discover what works for your specific situation.

When you make this shift, everything about the planning changes. People who base decisions on data, because they have access to real information, move forward with confidence instead of worry.

The questions become a tool for discovery rather than avoidance. There is no need to guess about property performance or care costs. The goal is simply to help people see their real situation clearly so they can make informed decisions.

This is why families who go through proper analysis become some of the strongest advocates for proactive planning. They do not feel like they were pressured into decisions, but rather feel like they were given the tools to understand their real options. So, where does this leave you if you are dealing with real estate challenges right now?

MOVING FORWARD

Whether it's property decisions, family conversations, or gaps in your data, the answer is addressing them one step at a time.

Families who need help with their real estate won't be served by avoiding the hard conversations about the future. And they certainly won't be served by making major decisions based on assumptions instead of real analysis.

What they need, and what every family deserves, are Real Estate Wealth Advisors who understand that proper planning requires real information about performance, costs, and options, combined with the time and expertise to help families understand what all that information means for their specific situation.

In the next chapter, we will explore the specific tools and systems that make informed real estate planning effective, the asset performance testing, and the tax analysis that turns overwhelming situations into clear choices for your real estate and your family's future.

SELF-ASSESSMENT: WHERE ARE YOU RIGHT NOW?

Take a moment to evaluate your current real estate situation. Check all that apply:

YOUR INVESTMENT APPROACH

☐ **Aspiring Investor**: You want to invest in real estate but haven't started yet.

☐ **Unhappy Investor**: You own properties, but they're causing stress or underperforming.

☐ **Indifferent Investor**: You own properties but rarely think about their performance or what you can do with them.

☐ **Happy Investor**: You're satisfied with your properties and actively manage them.

YOUR PROPERTY KNOWLEDGE

☐ You have properties sitting vacant because you're not sure what to do with them.

☐ You haven't changed the rent on your properties in several years.

☐ You know the rate of appreciation and dollar value of gain.

☐ You know exactly how your investment properties are performing relative to other investment options.

YOUR FAMILY PLANNING

☐ You worry about your children fighting over your real estate when you're gone.

☐ You're keeping properties "for the kids" but haven't asked if they actually want them.

☐ You have a trust, but it just says the kids "share everything equally" without specifics.

☐ You've had honest conversations with your adult children about inheritance expectations.

YOUR FUTURE PLANNING

☐ You have a clear plan for where you'll live if your current home no longer works.

☐ You know approximately how much care will cost if you need help.

☐ You've researched senior living options and their costs.

☐ You feel confident you have enough money to cover your future care needs.

☐ You've thought through the logistics of moving (what to do with your stuff, who will help).

YOUR DECISION-MAKING

☐ You avoid thinking about your real estate situation because it feels overwhelming.

☐ You often make assumptions about your properties without checking the numbers.

☐ You make real estate decisions based on actual performance data.

☐ You understand the tax liability when selling your properties.

REFLECTION QUESTIONS

- Which areas revealed gaps in your knowledge or planning?

- What assumptions are you making that you haven't verified with actual data?

- Where might you need professional guidance to get the information you're missing?

If you checked boxes that reveal uncertainty, such as properties you're unsure about, conversations you haven't had, or numbers you don't know, you're not alone. Most people discover they are making important decisions without all the information they need. The good news is that these gaps can be filled with the right tools and approach.

In the next chapter, we'll cover the tools you need—asset performance testing and tax analysis. Then in chapter 7, we'll put those tools to work inside the PLAN framework, a step-by-step process for evaluating your *Properties*, planning for *Longevity*, aligning your *Assets*, and setting *Next-generation* goals.

PART 2

A Different Way Forward

CHAPTER 6
The Right Questions

Most of us have heard a family member say, "Don't sell the real estate!" when talking about estate planning.

Maybe it was your parents or grandparents passing down what they learned from their parents. The advice usually comes with warnings you've probably heard before like, "You'll never find another property like this" or, "If you sell, you won't have land anymore."

So you keep the property because that's what you were told to do. It feels like honoring your family's legacy, being responsible, and doing what's right.

But what most people don't ask is, "Is it possible to buy a better property with the proceeds if I sold it?" or, "How exactly do you share land with your siblings?"

Most families don't think that far ahead because they assume it'll work out somehow. "All six of us will share it—we'll figure it out." But when you really think about it, who pays the property taxes on a shared piece of land? Who handles the maintenance? Who decides when to use it? What happens when one person wants to sell and the others don't?

The advice to never sell might have made perfect sense when your parents gave it, but families grow, needs change, and circumstances shift, and holding onto property simply because you were told to can create the exact problems that advice was meant to prevent.

Many families follow advice like "never sell" without ever stopping to question it. On the surface, everything appears in order—the property has appreciated, the expenses are manageable, and it feels like a solid investment.

But underneath, something else might be happening. Their real estate is quietly underperforming. They don't realize they might be leaving thousands of dollars on the table every year, money that could be improving their life, funding their retirement, or protecting their children's future.

And the part most people never think about is that holding the property until they die might actually be setting their kids up for the very conflict they've spent their whole life trying to avoid. The "never sell" advice that felt safe may be creating the perfect conditions for a family fight later.

When families see the truth, it's often the first time they realize the cost of doing nothing can be far greater than the cost of making a change.

The hard truth is that even if you've spent decades building wealth through real estate, without a way to measure its performance, how do you know you're maximizing its return? An even bigger impact on generational wealth is tax implications. Do you even know what your tax consequences are? Do you know what your options are? Are your decisions based on assumptions rather than facts?

In our experience working with estate attorneys, most families have some level of dispute after their parents pass away. More often than not, those disputes involve real estate. When you make your wishes clear about your real estate legacy, it lifts the burden and gives your family peace of mind, keeping them united when it matters most.

But clarity only comes when you know where you actually stand.

So before we look at the numbers and calculations, we need to address the belief behind the decision. Because if you're holding property based on old advice rather than your current reality, measurement alone won't help.

What makes the PLAN framework effective is this combination: strategic questioning that uncovers what you truly want paired with objective measurement that shows you where you actually stand. We'll walk through the full framework—Properties, Longevity, Assets, and

Next Generation—in the next chapter, but first, here's a glimpse of what it looks like when families put these pieces together.

FOR PROPERTY OWNERS: THE DISCOVERY SYSTEM

The questions we ask are designed to help you see your situation clearly, often for the first time. We believe that certain questions can help people discover that they need to see the world a little differently so they can achieve their goals.

These questions fall into two categories, and it is crucial that we address them separately:

CATEGORY 1: YOUR HOME—WHERE LIFE HAPPENS

Your primary residence holds more than just financial value. This is where your family lives, where memories are made, and where life unfolds. The decisions around your home should involve both your heart and your head.

You already know the fundamental question from chapter 4: Do you have a plan for when you can't stay home? But here is where the discovery system goes deeper. When we ask follow-up questions, the real picture emerges. Do you have a bedroom and bathroom on the first floor? Can you afford twenty-four-hour care if needed, which can cost around $24,000 per month?[8] Have you considered what "care at home" actually means, like strangers rotating through in shifts, equipment modifications, and safety concerns?

When people say, "I want to die in my home," they are often imagining something peaceful. But the reality is that 71% of Americans say they prefer to die at home, while only about 31% actually do.[9] The gap exists because accidents, illnesses, and the realities of end-of-life care often send people to hospitals or care facilities instead. Planning where and how you pass means having a plan before a

---

8 A Place for Mom, "How Much Does 24/7 Home Care Cost?" *2025 Cost of Long-Term Care and Senior Living Report,* 2025, https://www.aplaceformom.com/caregiver-resources/articles/24-hour-in-home-care.

9 Centers for Disease Control and Prevention, "QuickStats: Percentage of Deaths, by Place of Death — National Vital Statistics System, United States, 2000–2018," *Morbidity and Mortality Weekly Report 69,* no. 19 (2020): 611, https://www.cdc.gov/mmwr/volumes/69/wr/mm6919a4.htm

crisis forces one on you. That's what it means to be proactive.

This reality leads to another set of questions about timing. Is it easier to move when you are ill or when you are healthy? While you are both still here, or after your spouse passes? At seventy or at eighty? Do you want to be a burden to those you love the most, or would you rather be proactive?

When we ask these questions, people come to their own realization that yes, moving sooner makes sense. But until somebody asks the question, they stay hunkered down in outdated thinking patterns.

Once the decision to move is made, the physical logistics become the next challenge. Decades of accumulated possessions, each with its own story, create paralysis. Many older adults are byproducts of The Depression, so they didn't throw things away. They often say, "I'm going to use this one day." They didn't come from the microwave generation; they came from the generation of scarcity. Your kids might say, "Mom, you've got to get rid of all your crap," but those items represent your life, memories, and cherished treasures.

This situation is where professional help becomes essential. A Real Estate Wealth Advisor will partner with organizations like NASMM (National Association of Senior and Specialty Move Managers) that specialize in the physical and emotional aspects of downsizing and relocating. These professionals understand how to help you transition safely and smoothly.

For over ten years, we owned a senior move management company that helped more than

1,400 families downsize, declutter, and move. One truth became clear: The difference between a professional move and a family-managed move can be life-changing…sometimes literally.

For example, two sisters from wealthy families both decided to downsize and move into a retirement community at the same time. One hired our team who handled everything, from downsizing, packing, moving, and setting up the new home. Within thirty days, she and her husband were settled and enjoying their new life together.

The other sister decided to save a few thousand dollars and have the kids handle it. The family packed everything in boxes, moved it all, and left their elderly parents to figure out where it all went. About three weeks later, her husband tripped on one of those unpacked boxes and broke his hip. He did not survive more than thirty days after that.

You can probably see the difference in these moves. One sister invested in professional help, and both she and her husband are still healthy and enjoying life together. The other tried to cut corners and lost her husband as a result. Do you think a few thousand dollars saved was worth it? It's tough thinking about a widow having to live alone due to a decision to save a few thousand dollars.

Beyond the move itself, there is another question that catches people off guard: What do you do with your home after you move? This is where strategic questioning reveals options most people have not fully considered. This decision has massive implications for both your finances and your family's future.

Selling might be your best option if you have lived in the home for two out of the last five years. Under Internal Revenue Code Section 121, a married couple can exclude up to $500,000 of gain from taxation.[10] This is the best way to access money for care without paying tax.

The critical part is that if you move out of your home for three years and one day, it becomes an

---

10 26 U.S. Code § 121, "Exclusion of Gain from Sale of Principal Residence," Legal Information Institute, Cornell Law School, January 27, 2026, https://www.law.cornell.edu/uscode/text/26/121.

investment property. Sell it after that, and you are facing capital gains tax on every dollar of gain, potentially 20-30% in state and federal taxes,[11] depending on which state you reside in.

Renting is another option, but let's look at the math. When you calculate your rental income and subtract all expenses, property taxes, insurance, maintenance, and management, you get your net operating income. Annualize that number and compare it to the current value of the property. This gives you your capitalization rate, the measure of how well your asset is actually performing.

Once you have that number, you can compare it to other investment options. The question is not, "Should I sell or rent?" but rather, "How do I become the best steward of my wealth?" The only way to answer that is to measure the performance.

Then there is the option that no one ever wants, but can happen by default: keeping the home

---

11 Jared Walczak, "State Tax Rates on Long-Term Capital Gains, 2024," Tax Foundation, March 27, 2025, https:// taxfoundation.org/data/all/state/state-capital-gains-tax-rates-2024/.

vacant. This is the worst "option." A vacant home is a negative asset—often the largest asset you own that you keep pouring money into without getting anything in return. Insurance companies often will not cover vacant homes due to liability concerns.

But what about letting someone you trust live in your former home for free? Letting family live there sounds generous in the short term, but could create enormous problems in the long-term, which could turn into being a ticking time bomb for the family. We meet with families who deal with this exact situation all the time. For instance, the brother has lived in mom's house for twenty-five years. Now mom's in a care home and running out of money, so the daughter, who is the trustee, needs to sell the property. But the brother refuses to leave, and can you blame him? In his mind, it is his house. After twenty-five years, what else is he supposed to think?

Now the sister has to hire an attorney to get a writ of possession so the court can assign a sheriff to physically remove him and board up the house.

That's a devastating outcome that could have been prevented with better planning.

When you let family live in the home, they take emotional ownership. They often feel entitled. When you are gone and the trust says the assets must be shared equally, conflict becomes almost inevitable. The child who lived there for free resents having to share or leave, while the other children resent that their sibling received years of free housing while they did not get anything.

These decisions about your primary residence are deeply personal and emotionally charged. But when it comes to your investment properties, the questions shift from matters of the heart to matters of financial performance or generational wealth building. What could it look like if you unlocked wealth in these investment properties and repositioned it to what matters most to your loved ones? Most don't know what their options are.

CATEGORY 2: INVESTMENT PROPERTIES—WHERE YOUR MONEY WORKS

While your primary home is about life and legacy, your investment properties are about financial performance or generational wealth building. This is where emotion steps aside and the numbers do the talking. The question becomes simple: Is your property earning what it should? Or are you basing your decisions on comfortable assumptions without fully understanding your options?

What we hear most often when we ask that question is, "I'm keeping it for my kids."

That's a beautiful intention. You're thinking about legacy and passing something valuable to the next generation. But before we look at cap rates and cash flow, there's a more fundamental question worth asking: Do your kids actually want that specific property, or do they want the value within it?

Most people have never asked their children this question. They just assume. And while that assumption comes from a good place, it often creates challenges many have not anticipated.

If your kids want the property itself, that's one path forward. But if what they really want is the value—the ability to use that wealth in ways that serve their own lives—then holding the property until you die might not be the best strategy. Not for you, and not for them.

As we walk through the measurements in this chapter, keep that question in mind. The numbers will tell you whether your property is performing well, but only you can answer whether keeping it serves the legacy you're trying to create.

Most property owners know what they paid for a property and roughly what it is worth now. The rent comes in every month, so everything seems fine. But what many people do not realize is that net operating income, capitalization rates, and after-tax cash flow are the metrics that matter. The challenge is, most property owners have not been taught how to measure these. Once you understand them, you can see whether your real estate is truly working for you.

Let's start with the most important one: the capitalization rate. Take your annual net operating income (rental income minus all expenses—property taxes, insurance, maintenance, management, utilities, vacancy losses) and divide it by the current property value. This single number tells you the return your property is generating.

If the math feels overwhelming, don't worry, we've created a free calculator at danihara.com that does this for you. Just plug in your numbers and you'll see how your property is performing.

If your property is currently earning a 3% return, have you ever wondered if your money could be working harder for you? What are your options?

Here's one option: What if you could sell that property, defer all your capital gains taxes through a 1031 exchange, and reinvest it in another property earning 5% instead?

That extra 2% return makes a big difference. On a $2 million property, that's an additional $40,000 per year—and over ten years, that's $400,000 in increased cash flow, not even counting compound growth.

What we hear most often is, "I don't want to pay the capital gains tax." So they hold an underperforming asset to avoid a one-time tax bill, losing multiples of that tax bill in opportunity cost year after year.

Let's look at the math with a concrete example. Say you have a property worth $1 million that you bought years ago for $250,000. You are currently renting it now, and your net operating income is $19,000 a year. On the surface, that seems fine because you are making money, right? But what most people do not realize is that when you relate that income to today's value, not what you paid for it, that is only a 1.9% capitalization rate. With the Federal Reserve targeting inflation at 2% annually, a property earning less than that is not keeping pace, but actually losing ground.[12]

---

12 Board of Governors of the Federal Reserve System, "Why does the Federal Reserve aim for inflation of 2 percent over the longer run?" Federal Reserve, accessed December 2025, https://www.federalreserve.gov/faqs/economy_14400.htm.

Now here's where it gets interesting. If you sold that property and put the proceeds into a 5% return asset, utilizing a 1031 exchange, you would make $50,000 a year. That is over $31,000 more annually.

"But what about appreciation?" That is the question we hear most often. And it is a fair one, as real estate does appreciate. The question is, is your property the only one that appreciates? Keep in mind, the growth and appreciation are your growth of equity. Equity is usually realized when selling real estate or refinancing it. The challenge is that when you finally do sell, you are still facing that capital gains tax, just on an even larger gain.

This is where the 1031 exchange conversation usually starts. "Can't I just exchange into another property and avoid the tax?" Not exactly. A 1031 exchange defers capital gains tax rather than eliminating it.

The way to eliminate capital gains tax would be to hold real estate in your trust until you pass away, then your heirs receive the property at the stepped-up cost basis. If sold upon your death, there's no capital gains tax because the cost basis rises to the date of death value. Keeping the property in your name until your demise is one of the most tax-efficient strategies available.

The other consideration with a 1031 exchange is timing. Once you close on the first property, you have 45 days to identify replacement property and 180 days to close. One might think that forty-five days to identify a replacement property is too short and therefore not attainable. Using our proprietary 1031 exchange system, our clients have almost double that time. Our system, when executed properly, can create nearly ninety days by searching for your replacement property before you go on the market to sell your relinquished property.

Another thing to think about is that 1031 exchanges can be used for more than just deferring taxes. If you're keeping properties because you want to leave something for your kids, a 1031 exchange can help you reposition your wealth in ways that serve them better—both now and in the future. We'll explore those strategies in later chapters, but for now, just know that the question isn't only, "Should I defer the tax?" It's also, "Could this property be working harder for my family's future?"

Beyond the financial metrics, there are practical considerations that often get overlooked. Who manages the property day-to-day? Who handles the 2:00 a.m. call about a burst pipe? What happens when a tenant stops paying but will not leave—who oversees the eviction process? Do you understand your liability exposure if someone gets hurt on the property? And the biggest question: What happens to this management responsibility when you are eighty-five?

Every one of those questions has a cost attached to it. If you are hiring a property manager, that typically adds another 8-10% to your expense column. If you are managing it yourself, you are providing labor, which includes time, energy, stress, and possible contention with tenants—time that could be spent on other enjoyable aspects of your life.

The real question is, do you own your properties, or do they own you?

The only way to answer that honestly is to look at the numbers.

HOW TO MEASURE WHAT YOUR PROPERTY IS WORTH TO YOU

Strategic questioning only works when paired with objective measurement. Without numbers, you are just philosophizing, but with numbers, you have actionable intelligence.

Here is how we measure real estate performance. First, you calculate your Net Operating Income (NOI). Start with your gross rental income, then subtract everything, like property taxes, insurance, maintenance and repairs, property management fees, utilities if you pay them, and estimated vacancy loss. What remains is your NOI, the actual income your property generates after all operating expenses.

Next, you need to know what your property is worth today. Get a broker's opinion of value or commission a formal appraisal using current market comparables. The key is to use today's value, *not* what you originally paid.

Once you have those two numbers, you can calculate your capitalization rate. Take your annual NOI and divide it by your current market value. This single percentage tells you your property's return on equity. Now you can compare that to alternative investments and see how your real estate stacks up.

Now, if you are thinking about selling, calculate your tax consequences. We recommend you seek the advice of your tax consultant. If you'd like to use a calculator to estimate your capital gains tax in a general sense, head to danihara.com.

Once you know what the proceeds of your property sale could be, you can ask a different question. Not just whether the property is performing well financially, but whether keeping it serves what you want to accomplish with your wealth. We'll explore additional possibilities in the chapters ahead. Right now, simply focus on getting clear on the financial reality. That clarity makes better decisions possible.

When you run the numbers honestly, the results can be eye-opening. Many property owners discover that what they thought was a strong performer has actually been underperforming for years. In some cases, holding on just to avoid paying taxes has ended up costing far more in missed opportunities than the taxes themselves would have been. And what surprises most people is that the so-called "safe" choice, keeping the property, often turns out to be the riskiest one of all. But the numbers alone don't tell the complete story.

WHEN FINANCIAL PERFORMANCE MEETS FAMILY LEGACY

We've walked through the measurements like, cap rates, NOI, and after-tax proceeds. These numbers tell you whether your property is performing well financially. But there's a deeper question the numbers can't answer on their own: Is keeping this property the best way to serve the people you love?

Some people discover their property is performing beautifully and decide to hold it, while others realize it's underperforming and choose to reposition that wealth. And sometimes the numbers look fine, but they're managing properties because they believe that's what their kids need, without ever asking if there's a better way.

The measurements we've covered in this chapter give you the financial clarity you need. What you do with that clarity depends on what you want your wealth to accomplish. Not just for you, but for the people you care about most.

That's the conversation we'll have in the chapters ahead. Before we move forward, let's step back and look at what all of these questions are really asking.

THE QUESTION BEHIND THE QUESTIONS

All of these questions, about your properties, your future care needs, and your family dynamics, ultimately point to one fundamental question: Are you making decisions based on where you actually are, or where you think you are?

What we see most often is that people hold onto beliefs that made sense years ago, but don't always hold true today.

- "Real estate never goes down"—until it does.

- "I can't sell because of the taxes"—while losing more every year in opportunity cost.

- "My kids will figure it out"—until they're hiring attorneys to fight each other.

- "I'm not old enough to worry about this yet"—until a health event or crisis forces the decision.

The truth is, time changes everything—markets, tax laws, and family dynamics. The question is, are your decisions keeping up?

Remember, these questions aren't designed to make you feel bad about past decisions, but to help you see clearly so you can make better decisions going forward.

You cannot plan effectively for the future if you do not know where you stand today. And you can't know where you stand without honest measurement.

MAKING IT ACTIONABLE

Where do you start? Not with massive changes or dramatic restructuring, but with clarity.

FOR YOUR PRIMARY RESIDENCE:

1. Answer honestly: What's your plan when you can't stay home?

2. If you don't have a plan, start researching options now—care facilities, senior communities, aging-in-place modifications.

3. Consider whether moving sooner (while you're healthy) makes more sense than waiting.

4. If you decide to move, research senior move management professionals.

5. Understand the tax implications of selling your home at different time frames.

FOR INVESTMENT PROPERTIES:

1. Calculate the actual cap rate for each property.

2. Determine what the after-tax proceeds would be if you sold.

3. Compare current returns to alternative investment returns.

4. Honestly assess the management burden and your willingness to continue it.

5. Consider your exit strategy—because eventually, you will exit.

6. Consider whether keeping the property serves your goals.

   » Once you have your cap rate and performance data, ask: Does this property serve what I want to accomplish?

   » Are you holding it because it's your best investment, or because of what you believe your family needs?

None of this requires immediate action, but it does require immediate honesty.

Calculating your cap rate will not suddenly make your properties perform better, and acknowledging the challenges will not magically make your home easier to age in. But knowing the truth does give you options. Avoiding these numbers now means facing them later, usually when you are dealing with a health crisis or family emergency, with far fewer options. And if all of this feels like too much right now, know that you are not alone.

IF YOU'RE FEELING OVERWHELMED RIGHT NOW

If all these numbers, questions, and considerations feel a little overwhelming, don't worry! That reaction is normal. Many people feel that way when they first start looking honestly at their real estate situation. The "deer in the headlights" feeling is real.

What matters is that you do not have to figure this out alone. The measurements and questions we have covered in this chapter are designed to give you clarity. Start with one step, calculate one cap rate, and answer one question honestly. Progress comes from taking small actions, not from having all the answers at once.

In the next chapter, we will walk through the complete framework that brings all of these pieces together so you can see exactly where you stand and what your next move should be.

GET CLEAR ON THESE SIX QUESTIONS BEFORE THE NEXT CHAPTER

Take a moment to answer these questions honestly. If you find yourself struggling to answer clearly, that may be telling you something important about where you stand.

ABOUT YOUR PRIMARY RESIDENCE:

1. Where do I go if I can't stay home? (be specific):

- Do you have a written plan?
- Have you toured facilities or communities?
- Does your spouse agree with the plan?
- Do your children know what it is?

☐ I have a clear plan that my family knows about (2 points)

☐ I have some ideas, but nothing concrete yet (1 point)

☐ I haven't let myself think about this (0 points)

2. Do I have enough money?

Consider:

- Can you afford $24,000/month for 24-hour care if needed?

- Will your investment properties provide income or just appreciation?

- Have you calculated what you'll actually need?

☐ I've calculated what I'll need and know I'm covered (2 points)

☐ I believe I'm okay, but haven't done the actual math (1 point)

☐ I'm concerned, and I don't know how to figure this out (0 points)

3. What will you do with your home after you move?

Your options:

- **Sell** (best tax treatment if you've lived there two of the last five years)

- **Rent** (but do you know the actual return after expenses?)

- **Keep vacant** (worst option—worth a million but costs you money)

- **Let family live there** (creates entitlement and future conflict)

☐ I have a clear strategy based on the numbers (2 points)

☐ I'm leaning toward one option, but haven't analyzed it (1 point)

☐ I haven't decided because I don't want to face it (0 points)

ABOUT YOUR INVESTMENT PROPERTIES

4. Can you explain how your real estate performs compared to other investments?

Specifically:

- What's your capitalization rate on each property?

- How does that compare to what you could earn elsewhere?

- Are you making more or less than you think?

☐ I can answer this clearly with number.s (2 points)

☐ I have a sense of it, but haven't calculated the specifics. (1 point)

☐ I honestly haven't looked at this. (0 points)

5. Do you know your potential capital gains tax liability if you sold today?

For each property:

- Current value minus original purchase price = gain

- Federal and state capital gains tax on that gain

- After-tax proceeds available to reinvest

☐ I know these numbers for my properties. (2 points)

☐ I know some but not others. (1 point)

☐ I've been putting off looking at this. (0 points)

6. Would you rather be an active or passive real estate investor?

Think about:

- Has your property become a burden?

- Who manages tenant issues and evictions?

- Do you want to do this at seventy-five? At eighty-five?

☐ Active—I want to manage properties myself. (2 points)

☐ Passive—I want returns without the work. (1 point)

☐ I'm not sure what I actually want. (0 points)

WHAT YOUR ANSWERS TELL YOU

Your Score: _______ / 12

If you scored 10-12: You're ahead of most families. You have clarity on your situation and a plan in place. Now make sure your family knows your plans and that your numbers are documented and where they can find them.

If you scored 5-9: You have some clarity gaps. You're making decisions involving thousands, sometimes millions, of dollars based on assumptions rather than facts. The next chapter will help you get clear on where you stand.

If you scored 0-4: You're where most people are. These questions are hard, and it's natural to put them off, but the cost of waiting grows over time. The good news is you now know exactly what needs attention.

THE ONE QUESTION BEHIND ALL SIX

Are you making decisions based on where you actually are, or where you think you are?

Planning for the future becomes much clearer when you know where you stand today, and knowing where you stand starts with honest measurement.

If your head is spinning a bit from all the numbers, that's okay. You're not supposed to have it all figured out yet. What matters is that you now have the tools to see your situation clearly, and clarity is what makes confident decisions possible.

In the next chapter, we'll put these pieces together with the PLAN framework. You'll walk through Properties, Longevity, Assets, and Next Generation in a way that finally makes sense of everything you've been carrying. Your PLAN framework is where the path forward becomes real.

CHAPTER 7

The PLAN Framework—Your Family's Blueprint for Real Estate Wealth

This is the chapter we've been building toward. You've seen what's possible when families get this right, the roadblocks that keep people stuck, and the power of pairing the right questions with honest measurement. Now it's time to put it all together.

The PLAN framework is the roadmap that turns everything you've learned into action. By the end of this chapter, you'll know exactly how to evaluate your Properties, plan for Longevity, align your Assets, and set Next-Generation goals—step by step, in a way that finally makes sense.

But first, a question. Think about the last time you tried to have a serious conversation with your family about money or property...

How did it go?

If you're like most families, the conversation may not have happened at all. Or maybe it started, then got uncomfortable, and everyone changed the subject to something safer, like the weather or what's for dinner.

I've sat at countless kitchen tables with families who look different on the outside but share the same fears on the inside: The fear of saying the wrong thing. The fear of conflict. The fear of not knowing where to start. Talking about money and real estate feels impossible when there's no framework. But when families utilize the question based methodology with the right intentions, the defenses come down, people start to listen, and love finally finds its voice.

Maybe you feel the same way. When it comes to money, you might not know where to start, what to cover, or how to keep everyone from getting defensive when old wounds inevitably resurface.

We developed the PLAN framework to solve that lack of direction. It's a roadmap that transforms overwhelming decisions into manageable conversations that bring families together instead of tearing them apart.

Before we dive in, you should know that this isn't just another estate planning checklist or a financial worksheet you'll file away and forget. You're about to discover what you want for your family's future and how to get it without painful conversations that don't lead anywhere.

WHY YOU NEED ALL FOUR PIECES OF THE PUZZLE

You might be wondering how the PLAN framework differs from what your financial planner or attorney has already told you. The truth is, most professionals focus on their piece of the puzzle. For example, your financial planner looks at stocks and bonds, attorneys focus on the trust document, and your CPA thinks about tax consequences.

But who's looking at the whole picture? Who's helping you connect your real estate to your health planning, or your family dynamics to your financial goals?

This is where the PLAN framework comes in. It rests on four critical pillars—Properties, Longevity, Assets, and Next Generation—to form a complete foundation for your wealth and future.

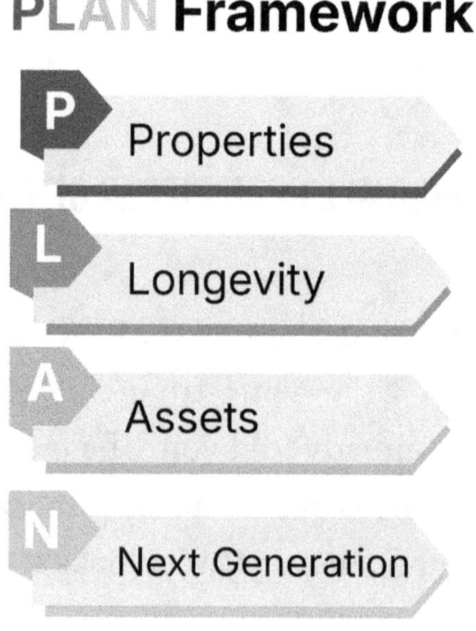

More importantly, the PLAN framework helps you discover what you want, instead of what someone else thinks you should do.

We believe in the saying, "Knowledge is what we know today, but imagination is what could be in the future." We can't change the past, but we can change the future, and your future starts with understanding where you stand right now.

Let's begin by talking about what happens when you commit to using this framework.

THE PROMISE OF PLAN

In the past, it may have been easy to file financial planning information away as something to tackle "someday." Often, that tendency is due to feeling overwhelmed and uncomfortable, but with the PLAN framework, you'll notice a different lens. When you use PLAN—sitting down with your spouse and answering the questions, calculating your numbers, and having that first conversation with your kids—a shift starts.

You'll stop feeling overwhelmed by your real estate decisions because you'll have clarity on exactly what you own and how it's performing. Nights will feel easier because you'll have a realistic plan for your future care needs, rather than hoping that everything will work out. Your family will thank you for having hard conversations now instead of leaving them to figure everything out during a crisis.

Most importantly, you'll move from being reactive to proactive. Instead of waiting for life to force your hand, you'll make decisions on your terms, while you still have options.

And as you may have noticed, the theme of this book is that the right questions change your future. Let's go through the PLAN framework together so you can start taking action.

PROPERTIES—WHAT YOU REALLY HAVE

Many property owners believe they know their real estate situation. They'll tell us, "I have three rental properties and my home," but when we ask them about the actual performance of those properties, the conversation becomes rocky.

Here's the first question of the PLAN framework: Do you know what your cap rate is for each property?

If you hesitated, you're not alone. Many property owners can tell you what they paid and roughly what it's worth now, but they can't tell you their cap rate, after-tax cash flow, or whether keeping the property serves their goals.

And if you think that to answer this question, you need to become an expert in real estate analysis, you don't. Most people just need to start with a simple question, like, "Is this property helping you build the life you want, or has it become one more thing to worry about?" When you know the answer to that, you know what to do next.

STARTING YOUR PROPERTY ANALYSIS

So where do you begin? The temptation is to freeze up, thinking you need perfect information, but you really don't. You just need to know enough to start asking better questions. Here's what to pull together for each property you own:

STEP 1: KNOW YOUR COST BASIS

What was the property originally purchased for? And if it was passed down, did you inherit it after someone passed (step-up in basis), or was it gifted while they were still alive (carry-over basis)? This is the starting point for understanding your potential capital gains tax. We'll discuss this more in chapter 10.

STEP 2: UNDERSTAND CURRENT VALUE

What could you sell this property for today? Not what you hope it's worth, but what the market will actually pay?

STEP 3: CALCULATE YOUR GAIN

The difference between your current cost basis and the current value lessens the cost of selling in your gain. If there's no gain, you could sell without tax consequences. But if you've owned property for any length of time, there's probably a significant gain. Keep in mind that your mortgage does not impact your capital gain.

STEP 4: UNDERSTAND YOUR TAX CONSEQUENCES

If you have a significant capital gain, then you want to know what the pain is if you fail to plan. What are the consequences if you don't do this right?

If there's a big capital gain, the question becomes:

"What happens if we don't plan this correctly?"

Knowing the potential tax hit helps you make a confident, informed decision instead of a costly one.

If you don't know the answer, that *is* your answer. A property you don't understand is a property that's controlling you instead of serving you.

Once you're clear on what your properties mean to you—both your primary residence and any investment properties—the next question becomes even more personal: How long will you actually be able to manage them?

LONGEVITY—PLANNING FOR YOUR REAL LIFE

Here's a conversation we hear almost daily: "Dan and Julie, I'm going to stay in my home for the rest of my life."

"We understand," is our response. "Just curious, what's your plan if one day, you can't do the stairs anymore?"

Silence.

This is the Longevity pillar, where we talk about not only how long you'll live, but also how you'll live as you age. This is where honesty is key, as the conversation revolves around what's ahead and making decisions while you still have choices.

THE THREE STAGES OF AGING

Whether we want to admit it or not, aging typically happens in three stages:

STAGE 1: THE GO-GO YEARS

You're healthy, active, and traveling. The house feels fine, maybe even a bit empty now that the kids are gone. This is when moving feels optional.

STAGE 2: THE SLOW-GO YEARS

Those stairs get a little harder each year. You find yourself sleeping in the recliner sometimes because getting to the bedroom feels like too much work. You start avoiding certain activities because they're becoming difficult.

STAGE 3: THE NO-GO YEARS

You need help with daily activities. Maybe it's just someone to handle the shopping and cleaning at first. Eventually, that help might include bathing, dressing, or managing medications.

These stages lead to the crucial question: Which stage are you in right now, and how long do you realistically have before the next stage? If you're an adult child, what stage is your mom in right now, and what's the plan when she needs help? When do you think she'll need assisted living care?

THE COST OF WAITING

The pattern we see over and over is that many families wait until Stage 3 of aging to make any changes. By then, *you're* not choosing your next move; it's being chosen for you, usually by your adult children in a moment of crisis after a fall or health scare.

Would you rather decide where and when your next move will be, or would you like to leave it to somebody else?

This is where the proactive person may say, "I want to decide where and when I'll go, so I'm going to start planning now." Following this scenario, the reactive person may say, "I'll figure it out when I have to."

But what the reactive person doesn't realize is that by the time they have to, they've lost most of their options. The communities they might have chosen have waiting lists, money they might have had could get eaten up by emergency care costs, as their family or possibly a social worker, scrambles to find any solution rather than the right solution. At this point, many have now become a burden to those they love the most.

CREATING YOUR LONGEVITY PLAN

You know what's interesting? When we sit down with families and begin talking about this, you can feel the room shift—everything gets quiet. It's like we're finally talking about the thing they've been avoiding for years. But what we've learned is that the families who face these questions head-on are the ones who get to control their own story.

So let's be honest with ourselves, because these questions we're about to go through aren't easy, but they are necessary.

Where will you go when you can't stay home anymore? Be specific. Have you toured senior living care options? Do you know what they cost? Does your spouse agree with this plan?

How will you pay for it? At the time of this writing, 24-hour home care costs can range from $4,000 to $12,000 per month, depending on location and level of care, with costs reaching $21,823 monthly at the national median.[13] "Assisted living ranges

---

13 "Cost of 24-Hour Home Care," UltimateCare, March 14, 2025, https://www.ultimatecareny.com/resources/cost-of-24-hour-home-care.

from \$4,000 to \$8,000,"[14] and memory care can reach nearly \$14,000.[15] Those costs will likely continue to increase. Do you have enough to cover them?

When will you know it's time? What's your trigger? A fall? When your spouse passes? When driving becomes unsafe? Would it be easier if you moved together while your spouse is around to help with the transition? Without a clear trigger, you'll keep pushing it off until it's too late.

These questions are meant to prepare you, and preparation starts with three concrete action steps you can take right now.

---

14 Susanna Guzman, "How Much Does Assisted Living Cost? A State-by-State Guide," aPlaceforMom, February 18, 2025, https://www.aplaceformom.com/caregiver-resources/articles/cost-of-assisted-living.

15 Taylor Shuman and Abby Altman, "Memory Care Costs in 2026," SeniorLiving, December 18, 2025, https://www.seniorliving.org/memory-care/costs/.

YOUR LONGEVITY ACTION STEPS

ACTION STEP 1: HAVE REAL CONVERSATIONS

Talk with your children realistically about whether they can care for you. Will they be able to help? Do they want you to move closer? Would they want you living with them?

Most people say, "My kids will take care of me." But the reality is that your kids aren't trained for this. They don't know how to lift, transfer, or provide medical care safely. Julie experienced this firsthand with her mom, where even simple tasks like helping with bathroom trips became sources of conflict and resentment.

ACTION STEP 2: RESEARCH YOUR OPTIONS

Know what's available at different care levels at retirement communities:

- Independent living: No care needed—safe environment, social support, activities, classes

- When you need some assistance: Cooking and cleaning

- When you need more care: Assisted living, when two of the six ADLs (activities of daily living) are needed—bathing, dressing, eating, toileting, transferring, and continence

- Memory care: dementia, Alzheimer's, and cognitive care

Then find out what these actually cost in your area.

ACTION STEP 3: DECIDE ON YOUR TERMS

The proactive person says, "I want to decide where and when I'll go, so I'm planning now." Be the proactive person. Start planning now.

By answering these questions now, while you're healthy and clear-minded, you give yourself and your family the incredible gift of clarity.

But clarity about where you'll live is only part of the equation. The bigger question is: How will you pay for it all?

ASSETS—YOUR COMPLETE FINANCIAL PICTURE

Picture this situation as if you're sitting across from your financial planner. You've just finished reviewing your portfolio—your stocks look good, your bonds are balanced, and your 401(k) is on track. You lean back in your chair, feeling pretty confident about your financial future.

Then you get asked the question: "How does your real estate fit into this plan?"

Silence.

"Well," you might say, "That's separate. That's my house and rental properties."

And right there, you've revealed the blind spot that costs families hundreds of thousands of dollars.

You see, we've all been trained to think about money in compartments. As we mentioned before, your financial planner handles investments, your CPA handles taxes, and your attorney handles the trust. But who's looking at how your real estate connects to everything else?

We believe that real estate isn't separate from your wealth picture because it *is* your wealth picture. Yet most families treat it like it's in a different universe from their other assets.

But real estate is not separate from your asset plan. This line of thinking is where families can miss enormous opportunities. Your real estate *is* an asset, and it's often your largest one. But families rarely include it in their financial planning because they don't know how to measure it against their other investments.

The good news is that when you learn to measure your real estate like any other investment, you'll finally see what you've really got, and what it could be doing for you.

BUILDING YOUR INTEGRATED ASSET PLAN

So how do you stop treating your real estate like it's in a different universe from your other investments? How do you actually bring these pieces together so they work for you instead of against you?

This is the plan we follow with families every day.

ACTION STEP 1: REVIEW YOUR INSURANCE COVERAGE

Long-term care insurance is your first line of defense because it reimburses you and preserves your wealth. Disability insurance works similarly, protecting your income if you become unable to work. Then there's life insurance, which serves a different purpose—while most people worry about leaving something for their kids, if they have life insurance, that's already taken care of, freeing them to focus on their own care needs.

Here's where you can ask yourself: Do I have these protections in place? If not, why not? If yes, when's the last time you reviewed the coverage amounts?

ACTION STEP 2: CONNECT YOUR ADVISORS

Connect your financial planner with your real estate wealth advisor. Together, they can create a holistic approach to planning your finances from today through the end.

Remember, not all financial planners are created equal. Find one who specializes in working with seniors and understands both the accumulation phase you've been in and the distribution phase you're entering. They should be asking:

- How long will your money last, given probable care needs?

- What happens if you outlive your projections?

- How does real estate fit into your income strategy?

ACTION STEP 3: CALCULATE YOUR TRUE POSITION

First, calculate your total net worth, including all real estate at current market values. Use what it's worth today, not what you hope it might be worth. Next, figure out what income you need to sustain your desired lifestyle. Be realistic and include everything from daily expenses to travel, healthcare, and those gifts you want to give the grandchildren.

Then ask yourself: Are my assets positioned to provide that income efficiently?

If your answer involves hoping for appreciation or assuming rents will increase, ask yourself: Is that really a plan, or am I just wishing things will work out? And while we're being honest with ourselves, we should also talk about the thing that stops more families from taking action.

THE TAX REALITY CHECK

When you sell investment property, there is usually a significant capital gain, which means significant tax consequences.

Think about it this way: You need to understand your cost basis, which is what you originally paid, or the value when transferred to you. The difference between your cost basis and what you sell for is your gain. And if there's gain, which there likely will be after years of ownership, you need to know what the pain is if you fail to plan properly.

What are the consequences if you don't calculate your capital gains tax correctly? If you use your brother's wife's sister, who's a part-time realtor who doesn't know how to do this, is that a good thing? Or do you need an expert, somebody that's never failed?

So, understanding the cost basis, the value at the sale, and the pain of selling—which is the tax consequences—you put that on the side and say, "That's the number I want to avoid."

And the way you avoid it is through a 1031 exchange.

This strategy allows you to reposition that property into something that better serves your goals without triggering that massive tax bill today. Understanding your cost basis will help you be able to control when and how you pay taxes.

Once you understand the tax implications, you can focus on what really matters, whether these properties are serving the life you want to live.

THE INVESTMENT PROPERTY QUESTION

If you have investment properties, the key question is: Do I need the income to sustain the life I desire?

If yes, we focus on making more money from those properties, but if not, we start planning for the next generation. This brings us to our final pillar.

NEXT GENERATION—BEYOND THE TRUST DOCUMENT

If you only have one child, this section is simple— everything passes to them with little to no disputes.

But if you have more than one child, consider that they're probably going to have different ideas about what should happen.

We ask families these questions:

- Are all your kids alike?
- Do they think alike?
- Do they act alike?
- Are they in the same economic stage of life?

Almost nobody says yes to all of these. We have three kids ourselves, and none of them are the same. Some parents can raise different people with different needs, desires, and lifestyles. Spouses of your children add more elements as well.

Knowing this, and knowing that 70% of families have some level of inheritance dispute, you need a plan that helps prevent those disputes before they start.

THE TRUST ISN'T ENOUGH

Most people believe that having a trust solves everything. But when your trust says "my three children share equally," how exactly do three people with different financial situations, emotional attachments, and life circumstances share real estate?

They don't, which leads to struggle.

One wants to keep it for sentimental reasons, another needs the money now for their kids' college, and the third lives across the country and wants nothing to do with managing property. There's often no timeframe for when to sell or clear instructions for handling disagreements.

This is why you need a complete family action plan.

CREATING YOUR FAMILY ACTION PLAN

STEP 1: UNDERSTAND THE REALITY

Accept that your children are different people with different needs. What works for one won't work for all. And remember, sometimes the challenges don't even come from your children—it's the in-laws offering their opinions about what's fair or what mom would have wanted.

STEP 2: HAVE INDIVIDUAL CONVERSATIONS

Ask each child separately: "When you inherit property, what would you want to do with it?" Don't ask them together initially; you'll get more honest answers one-on-one. This helps you understand their true needs before family dynamics complicate the discussion.

STEP 3: ADDRESS DIFFERENT CONTRIBUTIONS

If one child took care of you for years while others lived their own lives, acknowledge it. Consider whether equal distribution is the same as fair distribution. Have that conversation while you're alive to explain your reasoning.

STEP 4: CREATE CLEAR INSTRUCTIONS

Your trust needs to say more than, "share equally." It needs:

- timeframes for decisions,
- process for handling disagreements,
- clear guidance if someone doesn't cooperate,
- recognition of different contributions and needs, and

- clear designation of who the trustee is and what that means.

The person you name as trustee carries a significant responsibility. We see trustees who don't even know they're the trustee, or they know but feel paralyzed because the trust doesn't give clear instructions. Make sure your trustee understands their role and has the tools to succeed. If your parents own real estate, you'll want to be sure all properties are properly funded in a trust and may want to know who the trustee is.

STEP 5: CONSIDER PRE-INHERITANCE PLANNING

Through strategies like 1031 exchanges, you can divide properties while you're alive and keep them in your name until your demise. We'll discuss strategies in more detail in chapter 8. If you have children, you can help them with what serves their situation:

- The one needing income gets a cash-flowing property.
- The one seeking growth gets property in an appreciating area.

- The one wanting no real estate responsibility gets a Delaware Statutory Trusts (DST).

This way, you will make the decisions based on your values and their individual needs, rather than forcing them to figure it out while grieving.

Now that we've walked through each pillar, you might be wondering: How do all these pieces work together? Let's walk through the bigger picture.

BRINGING PLAN TOGETHER: THE CROSS FRAMEWORK

Picture a cross. The horizontal line represents time—your parents' generation on the left, your generation in the center, your children's generation on the right.

The vertical line represents resources flowing through the generations. At the center, where the lines meet, that's you, the decision-maker who determines how wealth flows to the next generation.

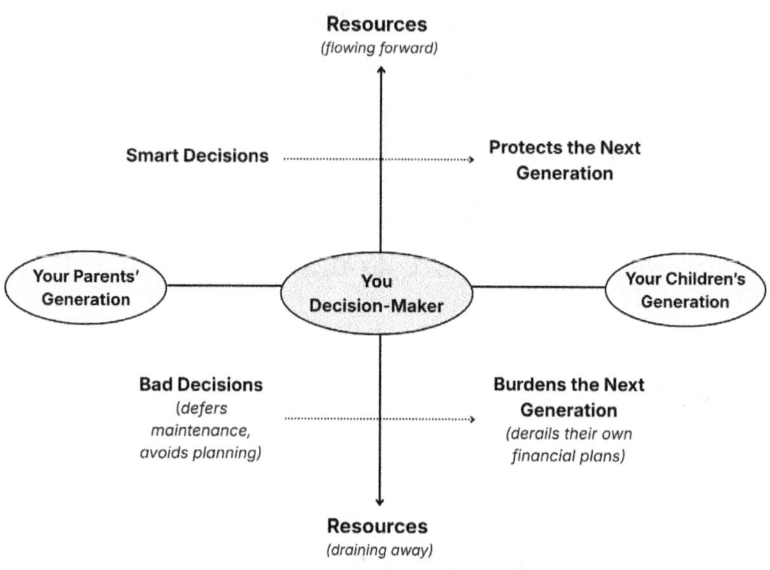

Every decision you make affects both lines. When you defer maintenance on a rental property, you're potentially leaving a burden for your children. When you avoid planning for your own care needs, there's a chance you're forcing your children to derail their own financial plans to care for you.

The PLAN framework helps you see these connections. When you understand your *Properties'* true performance, you can better plan for your *Longevity* needs. Then, when you make smart decisions about your *Assets*, you protect the

Next Generation from scrambling during a crisis. Each pillar influences the others—change one, and it ripples through them all. That's why we look at all four together, instead of in isolation.

Now that you understand how the pieces fit together, the question becomes: What are you going to do about it?

YOUR IMMEDIATE ACTION STEPS

Reading about the framework isn't enough. Here's what you can do in the next forty-eight hours:

STEP 1: THE REALITY INVENTORY

Take one hour and write down every property you own, its approximate value, and any mortgage balance. If you own rentals, then, as we illustrated in chapter 6, do the math, determine your capitalization rate, and see if it's worth keeping. Just write what you know. This simple act will reveal how much you don't know, and that's where growth begins.

STEP 2: THE FUTURE CONVERSATION

Have one conversation with your spouse about this question: "If one of us needed care and couldn't stay home, what would we do?" No need to solve this question at the moment, as it's a matter of starting the conversation. The conversation itself is progress.

STEP 3: THE CHILD CHECK-IN

Call one of your adult children and ask, "Have you ever thought about what you'd want to do with our properties when we're gone?" Listen to their answers without judgment. You might be surprised by what you hear.

These three small steps will teach you more about your real situation than reading a dozen books. They'll show you where the gaps are in your planning and where the potential conflicts might arise.

WHEN YOU HIT RESISTANCE

As you work through PLAN, you may hit resistance. Your spouse might say, "Why are we talking about this? We're fine." The kids will probably tell you, "Mom, Dad, we don't want to think about that." Meanwhile, that voice in your head keeps whispering, "I'll figure it out later."

When this happens, remember: 70% of families fight over real estate after parents pass,[16] long-term care costs can drain an estate faster than most people expect, and every family in crisis thought they had more time.

The resistance you feel doesn't have to do with planning, but rather with the core issue—facing mortality, acknowledging aging, and admitting life changes, whether we plan or not.

We believe that being scared means you need to do it anyway because your family's future is more important than your fear.

WHERE YOU GO FROM HERE

You now have a complete framework for thinking about your real estate wealth. You understand how

---

16 Williams, Roy, and Vic Preisser. *Preparing Heirs: Five Steps to a Successful Transition of Family Wealth and Values*. San Francisco, CA: Robert D. Reed Publishers, 2003.

Properties, Longevity, Assets, and Next Generation connect, and you have specific questions to ask and actions to take.

But the question now is whether you'll use it.

Will you be proactive or reactive? Will you make decisions on your terms or let circumstances decide for you? Will you have the hard conversations now or leave them for your family to struggle through later?

The choice is yours. It starts with a decision, and that decision starts now.

SELF-ASSESSMENT: YOUR PLAN READINESS

Before moving on with your day, answer these questions honestly:

For Properties

- Can I list all my properties and their current performance from memory? Yes ☐ No ☐

- Do I know my cap rate for each rental property? Yes ☐ No ☐

- Have I calculated the tax consequences if I sold today? Yes ☐ No ☐

For Longevity

- Do I have a written plan for when I can't stay home? Yes ☐ No ☐

- Have I researched actual costs for care in my area? Yes ☐ No ☐

- Does my family know my preferences for care? Yes ☐ No ☐

For Assets

- Are my properties integrated into my overall financial plan? Yes ☐ No ☐

- Do I know if my assets will provide enough income for my needs? Yes ☐ No ☐

- Have I considered tax-efficient strategies for repositioning wealth? Yes ☐ No ☐

For Next Generation

- Have I asked my children individually about what they want? Yes ☐ No ☐

- Does my plan account for their different life situations? Yes ☐ No ☐

- Have we discussed this as a family? Yes ☐ No ☐

If you answered "No" to more than half of these questions, you're where most families are, and exactly where you don't want to stay.

If you answered "Yes" to most of these questions, congratulations—In my experience, you're ahead of a vast majority of families out there. Now your job is to make sure your plan stays current, and your family stays informed. Life changes, laws change, and what worked five years ago might need updating today.

CHAPTER 8

What's Missing From Your Plan?

A financial planner called us one day and said, "Dan and Julie, I have someone who needs your help. She owns multiple properties, and her kids barely speak to each other. She's headed for a real problem."

We set a time to meet at the financial planner's office, where we met the ninety-year-old woman who told us about every accomplishment she'd ever had. She was a CPA, financially savvy, and had built a portfolio of eighteen properties over her lifetime. She was proud, and she should have been.

"My daughter's an attorney," she said. "She's my smart trustee who will figure it out when I'm gone."

We nodded and listened. Then we pulled out eighteen stacks of paper—one for each property—and spread them across an eight-foot table: tax records, property details, permits, and comparable market valuations. The table disappeared under the weight of decisions that would need to be made.

The daughter, sitting in the corner with her phone in her hand, looked up. She stared at the table, and her face changed. In that moment, the ninety-year-old woman finally saw what was coming and what it would mean for her family if she didn't act.

When this mother and her daughter saw the sea of decisions that faced them, the conversation shifted. Because intelligence isn't the same as readiness, and being smart doesn't necessarily mean you're prepared for the emotional weight of making decisions that will affect your siblings, your inheritance, and your family's future—all while grieving the loss of your parent.

This chapter is about the gap between the plan you think will work and the reality you run into when life gets messy. The moment when real people, emotions, and decisions enter the picture, your clean plan starts to wobble.

So what's the difference between being "smart" and being "ready"? We see two key missing pieces:

1. The mechanics—the practical, step-by-step actions that keep the plan from falling apart

2. The humanity—the feelings, family dynamics, and tough conversations that ultimately decide whether the plan succeeds or never gets off the ground

Because at the end of the day, real estate planning isn't just about properties, it's about people. In this chapter, we'll walk through both, starting with the mechanics of getting the right team and systems in place, then addressing the emotional side that no amount of paperwork can solve on its own.

WHEN SMART ISN'T ENOUGH

The ninety-year-old CPA believed her daughter's impressive credentials would be enough to help her sort through everything once she died. After all, her daughter was a smart and capable attorney. What more could you need?

What this mom *didn't* see was the burden she was placing on her named trustee.

When someone passes away and leaves eighteen properties behind, it can be assumed that the trustee only inherits real estate, but the truth is, they also inherit decisions that will make or break family relationships. Which property goes to which sibling? Who gets the one everyone wants? How do you divide something that can't be split?

People think that because their child is a doctor, attorney, or engineer that they'll figure it out. But the challenges left behind after death stem from emotions.

How do people make decisions when they're under stress? When it involves their money, inheritance, or sense of fairness? When old wounds from childhood resurface, like, "You were always Mom's favorite. You got the better deal. You never helped when they needed care."

The challenge is that intelligence doesn't always prepare you for emotional decisions. When feelings are running high—grief, stress, old wounds—even the most capable people struggle.

What the CPA didn't realize is that the dissemination and disbursement of wealth, especially real estate wealth, is a burden. When there are multiple properties and multiple heirs, somebody has to make decisions, and somebody else in the family might disagree and say that wasn't the right choice.

So what the CPA could have asked herself, and what every parent may consider asking, is: "No matter how smart they are, do I want my kids to *have* to figure all of this out?" That question leads to another: What prevents families from ending up in sticky situations with hurt feelings and conflicting opinions?

GETTING THE HUMANITY RIGHT

Through years of watching families try to keep their plans working over time, we've identified two foundational elements that can determine whether a plan succeeds or falls apart.

The first foundational element is what we call predetermining factors—the mechanics. These are the technical, legal, and financial structures that need to be in place. The second foundational element is the feelings component—the humanity. The emotional intelligence and family dynamics that no amount of paperwork can solve on its own.

Most families focus on one foundational element or the other. They either focus heavily on the legal documents and overlook the human element, or they believe good relationships will overcome any planning gaps. The challenge is that neither approach works on its own.

You need both, and you need them working together.

GETTING THE MECHANICS RIGHT

When we talk about mechanics, we're talking about making decisions now, while you're alive, healthy, and thinking clearly, rather than leaving your children to make those decisions while they're grieving.

The story of the ninety-year-old CPA with the smart, attorney daughter shows this factor clearly. After seeing all eighteen property profiles spread across the table, she started asking different questions.

"Is that what I want?" she finally said. "For my daughter to be forced into making decisions I should have made? For her siblings to argue with her about choices I could have clarified while I was here?"

That's when we started exploring her options. Through strategic questioning, we learned that her kids didn't all want real estate, but rather the value within it, and they wanted it in different forms.

One child needed a place to live, another wanted passive income, and the third wanted nothing to do with property management but would appreciate the financial benefit.

By selling several properties to buy others through 1031 exchanges, we could bless each child based on what would help them most, instead of making them all share something none of them wanted to manage together.

This example is what we mean by predetermining. Making decisions now so your family doesn't have to guess, argue, or damage their relationships trying to figure out what you would have wanted. But how do you actually make those decisions wisely?

THE TEAM THAT CONNECTS THE PIECES

Think of wealth planning like a beehive. The queen bee—that's you and your family—sits at the center. Around you are the worker bees: the Real Estate Wealth Advisor, tax consultant, estate attorney, financial advisor, insurance professional, trust officer, and property manager.

Right now, the missing piece is connection. Your tax consultant may not speak to your Realtor, and your Realtor doesn't talk to your financial advisor. They're all in their own silos, doing their jobs, but no one's connecting the pieces.

That's where the Real Estate Wealth Advisor comes in. We're the connector bee, and our job is to bring everyone together. We create a hub where all these professionals work in alignment, because we all have the same common goal: to protect the queen bee.

When bees work together in alignment, the hive thrives, producing abundance for both current and future generations.

Real Estate Wealth Hive

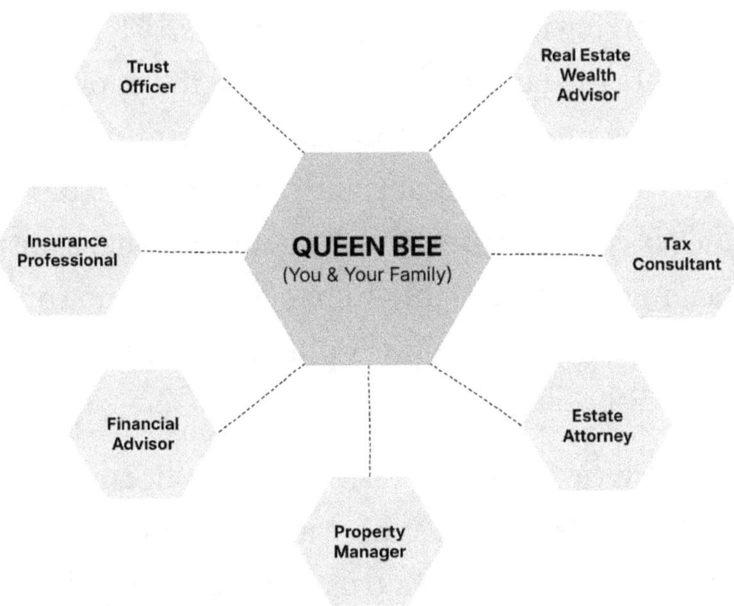

But let's be specific about what each of these professionals does and why you need them.

The Real Estate Wealth Advisor guides strategy on real estate. We create asset performance tests to make sure your properties are working for you. If they're not, we give you solutions and options. We're the ones asking the questions that help you discover what you truly want, then coordinating with all the other professionals to make it happen.

The Tax Consultant helps you understand the tax consequences that come with buying, selling, or transferring real estate. Selling a property typically triggers the largest tax bill because it can trigger capital gains taxes, depreciation recapture, and other taxes. Most importantly, they can calculate the tax consequences of each strategy: capital gains tax on selling outright, homeowner's exemption, 1031 exchange, and other options you may have at your disposal.

The Estate Attorney creates the trust documents and legal structures. Where it gets tricky is in the trust section. Having a trust that says, "My three kids share everything equally," isn't enough. Your attorney should work with your Real Estate Wealth Advisor to create specific instructions about what happens when your kids disagree, who makes decisions, and how disputes get resolved.

The Financial Advisor manages your liquid assets—stocks, bonds, and retirement accounts. The challenge is, most financial advisors specialize in liquid assets because that's where their expertise and compensation lie. This matters because for most baby boomers, real estate is one of their largest assets. If your financial advisor isn't considering real estate, they're only looking at part of the picture

The Insurance Professional protects you from liability and loss. Something we see all the time is people paying off their mortgage, then canceling their insurance to save money. What happens if there's a wildfire? An earthquake? A flood? They have nothing left. The insurance professional's job is to make sure the outside protects the inside.

The Trust Officer is typically your trustee—the person who steps in when you're incapacitated or after you pass away. This is the person who has to execute everything in your trust document. And if there's no clear plan, that person has the hardest job of all these professionals, which is trying to preserve family harmony while people fight over real estate.

The Property Manager keeps your rental income flowing and your properties performing. The reality is that property managers typically work on tight margins and manage many properties at once, so regular owner communication often falls by the wayside. They set it and forget it. If you want someone who stays engaged—conducting annual reviews, doing market assessments, and keeping you informed about your options—make sure to ask about that when selecting a property manager.

When all of these professionals work together, coordinated by a Real Estate Wealth Advisor who understands the big picture, your properties get positioned correctly, taxes get minimized, and your family gets protected. Beyond the professional team, though, you need systems for family communication.

FAMILY COMMUNICATION: BEYOND ONE CONVERSATION

Communication takes more than one conversation. Ongoing dialogue about expectations, inheritance, and decision-making is crucial.

The challenge is, most people struggle to communicate with their kids about wealth. We recently heard someone say, "My kids never talk to me, and I never talk to them." That's a problem, and at that point, it may be too late.

When communication has completely broken down, one option is to have the attorney contact the heirs directly. The attorney says the same things Mom would say, but because it's coming from a neutral third party instead of a parent with an emotional history, it's easier for the kids to hear.

While this works, it's better to start the conversations yourself.

Ideally, you're having conversations now while everyone's healthy, emotions aren't running high, and while you can explain your reasoning and ensure your family understands your intentions.

These conversations should cover:

- **The needs and wants of each heir.** Start with needs first. Do they have a place to live? What help would benefit them most? Then move to wants, which might include helping grandchildren, teaching them to build wealth, or creating opportunities they wouldn't have otherwise.

- **The difference between blessing and spoiling.** Many parents believe that helping their children financially means spoiling them, but the difference is in how you talk about it. You can say, "I want you to be a responsible adult and make your own mark in the world, *and* I want to bless you." It's an *and*, not an *or*.

- **The reality of their relationships.** Ask yourself: Are all my kids alike? Do they think

211

alike? Are they in the same economic phase of life? The answer is almost always no. When real money is involved—more money than they've ever had themselves—and they need to make decisions together, those differences become problems.

There's usually one "golden child" in the family. While the parents may not realize this, the kids know. They remember when one sibling stole their truck at age five, threw a baseball at their head, or got preferential treatment. The trauma that happened at five years old is a memory that can be held onto for the rest of their lives.

Out of respect to Mom and Dad, no one says anything while the parents are alive. But once parents are gone, those stories start coming out. Stories that were suppressed for fifty, sixty, or seventy years surface. And suddenly, siblings who seemed fine together are fighting over who gets what.

These repressed dynamics and tricky situations are why the conversation needs to happen now, while you can facilitate it, explain your reasoning, and ensure everyone feels heard. Once you've had those conversations, you need to make sure your plan stays current as life evolves.

KEEPING YOUR PLAN ALIVE AS LIFE CHANGES

Creating a plan isn't a one-time event because life changes, markets shift, and family dynamics evolve. Your plan needs to change with them.

That's why we conduct annual real estate plan reviews with our clients. And while it can be easy to think these reviews may fall only along properties, they're also about four key areas of your life:

- **Properties:** How are they performing? Are there any problems? Have you put more money into them? We measure performance again to see if you're okay with your current rate of return, or if you'd like to increase your income.

- **Family:** How's your health? How's it going with your spouse? How are Mom and Dad? How are the kids? Family dynamics change over time, and your plan should reflect those changes.

- **Health and Longevity:** Has your physical situation changed? Are you comfortable in your home? These questions get more urgent as time passes.

- **Dreams:** What do you want to see happen in the next five to ten years? This is where we help you think bigger than what you may have been conditioned to think.

This last key area is critical because many baby boomers and their parents grew up in an environment of scarcity. They came from the Depression, or they were kids during that time. Growing up, they learned one lesson over and over: never spend, always save, and always hold onto every dollar.

But now you're at a point in life where you realize, I can't take it with me. That's the aha moment.

We ask: "Do you believe you're going to run out of money?"

"No, I'll never run out of money."

"Okay, so money is good for the good it does. What good do you want to do?"

Most people have a hard time with that question.

So we ask it differently: "If you could have the most ideal life for you and your family—take all borders away—what would it look like?"

"Well, I want to travel the world and take my family to create memories."

"What's in the way?" we ask.

After a moment, they respond with, "I just haven't."

"Okay, so how about we plan? Where do you want to go?"

We take out a map and say, "Point to anywhere in the world you want to go. Why? Because you can do it. You have the financial ability to do it."

Then we ask questions that hit home to many of our clients—and these are kind of harsh: "Do you want to do this when you can walk, or when you can't? How many good summers do you think you have left?"

That question changes the conversation because it creates urgency without creating panic. You realize you don't have the luxury of unlimited time, so you need to use it better.

We tell them: "When you travel, fly first class. Why? Because what are you going to do with the money otherwise? Enjoy life."

We say this to remove the scarcity perspective and give from abundance. With abundance, what can you do? What could life look like for you and the loved ones you care about?

Many people of this generation have a hard time with that mindset shift. Very few actually live the big life while the majority live a life of scarcity, even when they don't have to.

The more conversations you have with a Real Estate Wealth Advisor who guides you through these mindset shifts, the easier it gets. Most financial planners aren't asking these questions, not because they don't care, but because their model focuses on asset preservation. So once you're clear on what you want to do with your wealth, how do you know when it's actually time to make a move on your properties?

PLANNING YOUR EXIT BEFORE YOU NEED IT

One of the biggest gaps in most people's planning is that they have no predetermined triggers for when to sell, exchange, or transfer properties.

So how do you know when it's time to sell?

First, you need to be clear on whether you have enough money to live the life you want. If you don't, you should be measuring your assets to see if you can make more money. If you do have enough, then the question becomes: Why are you holding onto properties you don't need?

The most common triggers for selling are:

- **Burden with the property:** The tenant left, didn't pay, and trashed the place. People get tired of the "Terrible T's"—Tenants, Toilets, Trash, and Taxes. That cognitive burden finally becomes too much.

- **Too much deferred maintenance:** The property needs so much work that it's overwhelming. At that point, the question becomes: Is it worth fixing, or should you sell as-is and reposition the money elsewhere?

- **Not enough income:** The property is underperforming compared to other investment options. You might be earning half of what you could elsewhere.

- **Change in circumstances:** The tenant's lease is ending. Should you rent it again or sell it? That decision point is when people start considering their options.

Anytime there's a problem with a property, people consider selling. That's the trigger we see most often.

But you don't have to choose between holding the property or paying massive capital gains taxes. Through a 1031 exchange, you can sell one property and buy another without triggering tax consequences.

Even better, you can exchange into something called a Delaware Statutory Trust (DST)—a professionally managed investment that currently provides around 5% passive income without any of the headaches of property management. This means no more tenant calls or broken dishwashers, only monthly income.

Most financial planners have access to DSTs but rarely mention them. The challenge is that their business model centers on liquid assets, while real estate falls outside that focus

But a Real Estate Wealth Advisor can unlock that wealth, coordinate with your DST provider, eliminate the capital gains tax, take away the burden of the property, and give you a 5% cash-on-cash return with no headaches. True passive income.

And when you're gone, DSTs can be divided easily among your kids while real estate has to be sold. But with a DST, we've already done the repositioning, which is part of the pre-inheritance plan. This brings us to the final critical component:

how you transfer wealth to the next generation in a way that keeps your family together.

BLESSING YOUR FAMILY WHILE YOU CAN STILL CELEBRATE TOGETHER

When it comes to passing wealth to your children, you have a choice to make, and that choice determines whether your real estate brings your family together or tears them apart.

You have two options:

Option 1: Create a plan before you die.

Option 2: Wait until you die and let the cards fall where they may.

Active wealth transfer strategies are about making decisions now—while you're still here to explain your reasoning, ensure everyone understands what's fair, and prevent conflicts before they start.

Here's how it works:

Let's say you don't need the income from your investment properties to sustain the life you desire.

Instead of keeping them until you die, you could sell them through 1031 exchanges and allow your children to be part of the selection committee for the replacement properties.

They get to predetermine their inheritance by helping choose what they'll eventually receive. But the key here is, you're not actually transferring the wealth yet, but rather the decision.

The properties stay in your name until you pass away. When that happens, your children receive them tax-free through a step-up in cost basis. No capital gains tax, or fights about who gets what, because those decisions were made years ago with your guidance.

That's what active wealth transfer looks like. You're planning together now instead of leaving it all for later. But what if there's another way to think about this? What if your children don't need another property to manage and instead just need help getting into their first home?

USING YOUR WEALTH TO HELP YOUR CHILDREN BUILD THEIR OWN

In the 1980s, the typical first-time homebuyer was twenty-nine years old. Today, they're thirty-eight.[17]

Our kids aren't doing anything wrong. The math just doesn't work the way it did for us. Think about it, most young people today are carrying student loans we never had to deal with. Housing costs have grown so much faster than incomes, and honestly, where would they have learned about building wealth? We didn't teach it in schools, and most of us didn't talk about it at the dinner table.

So here they are, doing the best they can with what they know, paying $3,000 or more every month in rent. That's money that could be building their future, but instead it's building someone else's wealth. And the hard part is, they don't see another way.

---

17 Jing Feng and Christine Romans, "Many First-Time Homebuyers Are Pushing 40 as Millennials Wait in Vain for a Better Market," NBCNews.com, April 18, 2025, https://www.nbcnews.com/business/real-estate/many-first-time-homebuyers-are-pushing-40-millennials-wait-vain-better-rcna201786.

What can be hard for parents to realize is that if they're going to give their kids money when they're gone anyway, why wait?

Let us tell you about a grandmother who changed her granddaughter's entire financial future with one decision.

THE TALE OF TWO FRIENDS: ONE GIFT, TWO DIFFERENT FUTURES

Two young professionals moved into the same building. They had the same jobs, income, and monthly housing payment of about $3,000. But one had a grandmother who understood wealth building, and one didn't.

One grandmother had an investment property she was tired of managing. Through a 1031 exchange, she sold it and used part of the proceeds to put $100,000 down on a $500,000 condo. The key is that she co-owned it with her granddaughter—20% for grandma, 80% for the granddaughter.

That granddaughter took out a mortgage for her portion and started making payments. This was the same monthly cost as her friend, who was renting in the same building.

Fast forward thirty years. The friend who rented is still paying rent and has a zero dollar net worth. The only difference now is that her rent *doubled* because rent always goes up. But the granddaughter owns a property worth $1.2 million free and clear. Grandma passed away years ago, and that 20% ownership transferred to her tax-free through the stepped-up basis.

THE PRINCIPLE OF COMPOUNDING: WHY CO-OWNERSHIP BUILDS WEALTH

We believe that wealth isn't built overnight, but over time. Your returns build on themselves, year after year.

Look at those two friends again. The renter's thirty years of payments built wealth for someone else— her landlord. She'll never see that money again. But the other friend's payments built equity for herself with the help of her grandfather. After twenty years, she had $400,000. Over the next ten years, she added another $800,000. None of it would have been possible without her grandmother's decision to co-own that property. That $100,000 down payment and the 20% ownership stake gave her granddaughter a seat on the wealth-building train she couldn't have boarded alone. When grandma passed, that 20% transferred tax-free.

Money grows slowly at first, then suddenly accelerates, which is the power of compounding.

The hard truth is that your kids can't get on this wealth-building train without help. It's not that they're lazy or irresponsible, but instead they're facing a completely different economic reality than you did. And every year they wait, they miss more of that compounding growth.

HOW THIS STRATEGY SERVES BOTH GENERATIONS

Think about what helping your child into homeownership this way accomplishes:

- **For you:** You get out of a burdensome property without paying capital gains tax. Through the 1031 exchange, you defer all those taxes while repositioning into something that helps your family.

- **For your child:** They get into homeownership they couldn't achieve alone. They lock in their housing costs for thirty years while their renting friends watch their costs rise every year.

- **For your legacy:** You get to see your children secure and building wealth while you're alive to guide them. No wondering if they'll make good decisions with their inheritance because you're helping them learn now.

THE QUESTIONS THAT MATTER

Ask yourself these questions:

- Do I believe money is good for the good it does? If yes, what good is it doing sitting in an underperforming property?

- If my children are going to inherit from you someday, wouldn't it make sense to help them now, while I can guide them and see the difference it makes in their lives?

- If my kids are paying $3,000 in rent, wouldn't I rather see that $3,000 building equity?

MAKING IT WORK: THE MECHANICS

Here's how families are using their real estate to help the next generation build wealth:

- **Identify the right property:** Look at your properties and ask, which one should I take action on first? Maybe it's the rental that's become a burden or the one that's underperforming.

- **Execute a 1031 exchange:** Sell without triggering capital gains tax.

- **Partner with your child:** Use the proceeds for a down payment on a property they'll live in or near them.

- **Structure it smart:** You maintain ownership percentage until you pass, when it transfers tax-free.

- **Let compound growth work:** Your child builds equity while you're alive to see it.

The best part is that you're not giving them a handout. They're still making the mortgage payments and being responsible. You're just giving them what every previous generation had, which is a chance to own instead of rent.

We've watched this strategy transform families. Instead of the 70% who fight over inheritance, these families are building wealth together. The kids understand money because they're managing it, and the parents see their values being passed on in real time.

Most importantly, you're solving tomorrow's problem today. Your children won't be part of today's typical first-time homebuyer age statistic. They'll be building the same kind of wealth you did, only with a little help getting started, exactly like most of our generation got from our parents.

Because at the end of the day, watching your kids pay rent when you have the ability to help them build equity is watching opportunity slip away, month by month, payment by payment.

The question isn't whether to help them, but whether you'll help them now, when compound growth can work its magic, or wait until you're gone and hope there's enough time left for them to build something meaningful.

As proactive believers, there's nothing more proactive than securing your children's financial future while you're still here to celebrate it with them.

But all the legal mechanisms in the world won't save your family if you don't address what really tears families apart: the feelings.

WHEN LEGAL DOCUMENTS MEET FAMILY EMOTIONS

Now we need to talk about the second critical component. Remember the ninety-year-old CPA's daughter staring at those eighteen properties? What she was dealing with were emotions.

All the professional teams, communication systems, and legal documents in the world won't save your family if you don't address the emotional side of wealth transfer.

Here's what we know about feelings and family wealth:

The trustee has the hardest job

Their job is to divide the assets evenly among all heirs stated in the Trust Document. What if one wants to sell and another doesn't? That's where the problem finally arises. The trustee is responsible for executing the written wishes stated in the trust. What if one does not agree? What if one doesn't want to leave the house? What do you do?

Intelligence doesn't equal emotional readiness

Being a doctor, attorney, or CPA doesn't prepare you for the emotional weight of inheritance decisions. These challenges revolve around how people make decisions under stress, when emotions are running high, and money, fairness, and old wounds intersect.

Parents see what they want to see

You may see your kids laughing, texting in the family group chat, or hugging at the door when they leave, and you think they're close. They'll figure it out and would never hurt each other.

But what you don't see is what's been buried out of respect for you. The small wounds, quiet comparisons, and unspoken hurts that never got resolved because no one wanted to upset Mom and Dad. You're the glue holding it together. When you're gone, those old feelings don't stay buried.

Fairness is about feelings

You can divide everything equally on paper, but your kids may not see it that way. One child might have spent years caring for you while others lived their own lives, another may have gotten financial help when times were hard, and sometimes, there's that one who's always felt like the favorite. Fairness runs deeper than any spreadsheet can show.

That's why predetermining factors alone aren't enough. You also need to acknowledge and address the feelings.

The conversation might sound like this:

- "I know you took care of me for the last five years while your siblings lived across the country. That matters to me, and I want to acknowledge it in how I structure my estate," or

- "I helped you financially when you were going through your divorce. I don't want your siblings to resent that, so let me explain my thinking and make sure everyone understands," or

- "This property might seem like the better one, but here's why I'm structuring things this way…"

These conversations are hard. They require vulnerability, honesty, and the willingness to address tensions that may have existed for decades.

But having them while you're alive means your children don't have to guess what you meant, wonder whether you were being fair, or argue with each other while trying to interpret your intentions.

The predetermining factors handle the mechanics, and the feelings component handles humanity.

You need both. Yet even after hearing all this, most people still don't act. What's stopping them? Usually, it's one of these common myths.

THE MYTHS THAT COST FAMILIES MONEY AND PEACE

Before we move forward, we need to address the misconceptions that can prevent families from implementing these critical components.

Myth 1: "I can't sell real estate—my mom said to keep it in the family."

We address this through questions: What did your mom really mean? Did she mean to keep this physical property, or keep wealth in the family?

Would your mom want you to have more money or less money? If keeping this property gives you x, but selling and repositioning gives you 3x, would Mom want that?

The answer is almost always yes. Once you realize that "keeping it in the family" means keeping wealth in the family—not necessarily the exact same building—you can start making strategic decisions.

Myth 2: "In order to preserve tax benefits, I have to keep it until I die."

This misconception exists because many people don't know about 1031 exchanges. They believe their only options are to keep the property or pay massive capital gains taxes.

The truth is, there are mechanisms that allow you to sell, reposition wealth, and avoid taxes. You just need to know they exist and work with professionals who understand them.

Myth 3: "My kids will figure it out. They're smart."

Intelligence isn't the issue. The issue is the emotional burden of making decisions that affect siblings, during one of the most stressful times of their lives, without clear guidance from you.

Yes, your kids might figure it out. But is that what you want? For them to spend months or years in conflict, hiring attorneys, damaging relationships, trying to guess what you would have wanted?

Myth 4: "I don't want to spoil my kids."

The difference between blessing and spoiling is in the conversation. You can say: "I want you to be responsible. I want you to make your own mark in the world. And I want to bless you with what I've built."

It's not an either/or. It's both.

Most people see it as: "Either I'm going to bless you, or I'm going to spoil you." It doesn't have to be that way.

Myth 5: "We thought our family was perfect."

We believed our family was perfect too, until our parents got ill. Some of the kids had the time to help—cleaning the house, mowing the lawn, handling the day-to-day needs. Others were juggling full, busy lives and simply couldn't do as much. At first, everyone tried to ignore the imbalance, but resentment has a way of growing in the dark.

Over time, old hurts, past arguments, and the perception of favoritism began to surface, and the cracks in the family only deepened.

That's one of the biggest challenges. The misconception that your family is immune to the 70% statistic because your kids love each other.

They might love each other, but when money is involved, love doesn't always translate into agreement.

MOVING FROM UNDERSTANDING TO ACTION

You've now learned about professional teams, communication systems, monitoring processes, exit strategies, legacy implementation, and the feelings component that ties it all together.

The question is: Are these components in place for you?

Take a moment to assess where you stand. The self-assessment below will show you which areas need attention and which you've already handled well.

DO YOU HAVE THESE FIVE PIECES IN PLACE?

Answer these questions honestly:

PROFESSIONAL TEAM

☐ Do you have a Real Estate Wealth Advisor who coordinates your overall strategy?

☐ Do your professionals (attorney, CPA, financial advisor) communicate with each other?

☐ Do you have a tax consultant familiar with 1031 exchanges and real estate strategies?

☐ Does your financial advisor understand how your real estate fits into your retirement plan?

☐ Do you have adequate insurance coverage on all your properties?

FAMILY COMMUNICATION

☐ Have you had honest conversations with your adult children about inheritance?

☐ Do your children know what to expect, and have you explained your reasoning?

☐ Have you addressed any past issues that might surface after you're gone?

☐ Can your family discuss money and real estate without conflict?

☐ Have you acknowledged different needs and contributions among your children?

ASSET MONITORING

☐ Do you conduct annual reviews of your real estate performance?

☐ Do you know your cap rate for each investment property?

☐ Have you reassessed your properties within the last 12 months?

☐ Do you have a system for tracking property performance?

☐ Do you regularly discuss your real estate with your professional team?

EXIT STRATEGY

☐ Do you have predetermined triggers for when you'd sell or exchange properties?

☐ Do you understand your options for repositioning real estate without taxes?

☐ Have you explored passive income alternatives like DSTs?

☐ Do you know what you'd do if a tenant leaves or a property becomes burdensome?

LEGACY IMPLEMENTATION

☐ Have you created a plan for transferring wealth while you're alive to guide it?

☐ Do your children understand how they'll receive inheritance, and when?

☐ Have you considered pre-inheritance strategies like 1031 exchanges with selection committees?

☐ Does your trust have specific instructions beyond "share equally"?

EMOTIONAL COMPONENT

☐ Have you acknowledged feelings about fairness among your children?

☐ Have you addressed any guilt or concern about "spoiling" versus "blessing"?

☐ Are you comfortable having hard conversations about your legacy?

☐ Do you recognize the emotional burden your trustee will carry?

SCORING

If you checked fewer than fifteen boxes, you have significant gaps in your planning. The good news is you now know what needs to be addressed.

If you checked ten to twenty boxes, you're ahead of most families, but there are still critical areas that need attention.

If you checked more than twenty boxes, you're in excellent shape. Your job now is to maintain these systems and make sure they stay current as your life changes.

In the next chapter, we'll focus on the first step you can take towards deciding whether you're going to make your own decisions or let life make them for you. Before you can implement any strategy, assemble any team, or have any family conversation, you need to shift your mindset from reactive to proactive. Because understanding the framework is valuable, but taking that first step is what changes your family's future.

PART 3

From Understanding to Action

CHAPTER 9

The First Step–The Question Nobody Wants to Ask

Since you're reading both my and Julie's stories, I wanted to clarify that this next one is from me (Dan). My mom kept falling. At first, it was just once in a while, but then it became regular. My dad would try to pick her up, but he couldn't do it anymore. Eventually, the ambulance started coming to the house so often, the fireman and Emergency staff suggested they move to a safer environment.

Some of my siblings said, "Let's bring in help," and others volunteered to clean the house and do the yard work themselves. Out of six kids, there were different opinions about what should happen. The family was divided, and resentment began to build.

The problem with my mom's situation was that we waited too long to ask the hard questions. What happens when Dad can't lift Mom anymore? Who provides daily care? How does this affect each sibling? Some have more time than money, others have more money than time.

By the time we finally faced these questions, it was almost too late. Mom and Dad had already gone through months of unnecessary danger and family tension that could have been avoided if we'd just dared to ask these questions earlier.

Now, we see this same pattern with almost every family we help. They recognize that strategic questions work better than giving advice, and they can see how the right questions could completely change their situation. But once they finally see the full picture, they freeze.

They freeze because that first question, the one that matters most, means facing something we all work pretty hard to avoid: the truth that we're getting older and that our health will decline. Life is going to change whether we make a plan or not.

WHY WE FREEZE UP

When it comes to your home, the challenge is accepting that there will be a time when you'll be a burden to someone else if you don't create a plan.

Change is inevitable. Are you going to direct that change or let it direct you?

We hear it all the time: "I'm never leaving my home. I'm staying until I die." Saying it doesn't make it true, but what it does guarantee is that when change comes, someone else will make your decisions for you.

For investment properties, the challenge lies in being unintentional with real estate. It's easy to do nothing.

You tell yourself the property is appreciating, parents told you never to sell, paying taxes is out of the question, money isn't being lost, and you have a good tenant. So why rock the boat?

The thing is, there are five ways to build wealth with real estate. It can be easy to only ride the appreciation train and forget that investment properties should generate income and maximize wealth over time. Taking the easy route is rarely the best path because the cost of this path creates bigger problems tomorrow.

THE FIVE PILLARS OF BUILDING REAL ESTATE WEALTH

There are five key pillars to building wealth with investment properties. Most people only know about one, maybe two, and that's completely understandable. No one ever taught us there were five ways to build wealth through real estate.

1. CASH-ON-CASH RETURN

What is your cash doing for you?

If you invested a million dollars of cash into a property, how much cash is coming back to you every year? We measure this through an asset performance test and a capitalization rate, which is your cap rate.

The difference between a cash-on-cash return and a capitalization rate is that a cap rate assumes you paid all cash for the property, while a cash-on-cash return looks at what's really happening when you have a mortgage. The cash going out is the money you put down and the mortgage you're paying every month. What matters is how much is coming back compared to what you're putting in.

We believe astute investors are always measuring one asset against another, asking themselves, "If I sold this and bought that, would I be better off?"

2. APPRECIATION—THE ONE MOST PEOPLE SEE

Properties typically appreciate over time. In fact, most of our clients see building wealth in only appreciation and don't see the other four.

They tell us, "Yeah, I bought it in 1965, and look how much it's worth!" And that's great if you bought it decades ago. But what's changing is that properties don't always appreciate anymore.

We also have clients with condominiums bought ten years ago that are worth less today than what they paid because new developments came in, blocked their view, and were cheaper. Or maintenance fees doubled in three years, going from $400 to $800 a month.

Nobody expected inflation to hit like it has these past five years, and with it came insurance rates that increased exponentially. When you combine those two factors with aging buildings that need more maintenance, you get properties that are worth less now than they were ten or twenty years ago. This is shocking to people because they've only ever seen real estate go up.

In our first fifteen years in this business, real estate always went up. We never saw it go the other direction. But that's not the world we live in anymore, especially when you look at older condominiums where the maintenance fees have gotten out of control.

3. DEPRECIATION—A TAX BENEFIT MOST PEOPLE DON'T REALIZE THEY HAVE

The IRS acknowledges that rental properties wear out over time. Because of that, the government gives you a tax deduction every year. You don't spend the money to get this deduction because it's a paper expense that lowers your taxable income.

This is a benefit while you're building wealth because it reduces your taxes, and less taxable income means less tax to pay.

When you sell the property, the IRS wants some of that deduction back. This is called depreciation recapture, and it's taxed at 25%.

So depreciation helps you now, but you'll pay some of it back later if you don't do a 1031 exchange. Most people who say, "I'll just sell and pay the tax," don't realize this recapture even exists, and that's not their fault as no one explained it to them.

4. LEVERAGE—BUILDING WEALTH ON SOMEONE ELSE'S MONEY

Leverage means borrowing money to buy an asset. What's remarkable about real estate is that there aren't many assets you can buy today that build wealth where you only need to put down 25%.

Think about it, you put $250,000 down on a million-dollar property. In ten years, if that property becomes worth $2 million, you still only invested $250,000 of your own money.

Assuming the tenant's rent covers the mortgage payment, you've built a million dollars of additional wealth using the bank's money. That's the power of leverage.

5. THE 1031 EXCHANGE—KEEPING WHAT YOU'VE EARNED

This last pillar allows you to defer or eliminate your capital gains tax when you sell an investment property.

As we always tell our clients: It's not just what you make that matters, but what you keep.

Understanding how much you get to keep and how you can keep more of your money makes all the difference between building wealth and moving money around.

THE PROBLEM WITH ONLY KNOWING ONE PILLAR

Most of our clients come to us only thinking about appreciation. They bought a property, it went up in value, so they think they're doing great. But they're leaving four other wealth-building opportunities on the table.

When you understand all five pillars, you can make informed decisions about which properties to keep, which to sell, and how to structure everything to maximize your wealth while minimizing your tax burden.

Once you understand all five pillars, you start to see your properties differently. You can finally answer the question: Is my real estate truly working for me, or have I been settling for less than what's possible?

We believe that when you know all your options, you make better decisions, and better decisions lead to the life you want to live.

WHAT'S AT STAKE

Let's talk about what costs for your home and investment properties mean for your family.

For your home: Without a plan, a crisis can control your future. Your declining health already weighs on your family and adds impossible decisions to their burden. There probably aren't any good options at this point besides feeling stressed and guilty.

For investment properties: When you don't plan, every property becomes a question mark. Who gets what? Who decides? Who manages it? You won't be around to answer. What you intended to be a blessing becomes the weapon your kids use against each other.

We've watched this unfold with too many families. Parents work their whole lives to build something to pass on, but without a plan, that gift becomes a burden. Five properties, three kids—the math doesn't work. Who gets what? These are the questions that pull families apart when there's no clear direction. But it doesn't have to be this way.

BEFORE THE NUMBERS: GETTING HONEST WITH YOURSELF

Twenty years of helping families taught us how to break down overwhelming decisions into simple conversations through strategic questions about your home and investment properties. But before we go over these sections, let's talk about the difference between being ready to ask and knowing what to ask

GETTING HONEST WITH YOURSELF

The first thing you have to do is be honest with yourself. And that's usually the hardest step, because every one of us is in denial about something. So the real question becomes: How do we break through that denial? How do we reach that place where we can finally tell ourselves the truth?

Before we walk through the specific questions, there's something we need to address first.

THE EMOTIONAL SIDE OF PROPERTIES

Properties can be more than numbers on a spreadsheet. That rental house might be the first home you bought as newlyweds, or it may be that the cabin is where your kids learned to fish. These emotional connections matter, and the PLAN framework doesn't ignore them.

The question becomes: Are you keeping this property for the memories or for the money?

Both answers are valid, but you need to know which one is driving your decision. If it's memories, wonderful—just understand that there is a cost to those memories. And if it's money, then we need to make sure the property is delivering what you need.

Remember, there's no wrong answer here, as these questions come from curiosity instead of judgment.

With that settled, here's how to approach the conversation.

Block out some time when you can sit down somewhere comfortable, maybe pour yourself something to drink, and give this your full attention—two hours minimum, as this conversation deserves that.

If you have a partner, have the conversation together since both perspectives need to be heard. We've seen too many situations where one spouse makes all the decisions and the other feels left out of their own future.

Then think about your adult children as they see things you might not want to see. When they're constantly saying, "Mom, Dad, we're worried about you in that big house," maybe it's time to listen.

Overall, our advice is to have the conversation with your partner first. Get clear on what you both want. Then, and only then, bring in the kids if you want their input.

If you own both a home and investment properties, we'd actually start with the investments because it is often less emotional than our primary residence. Dealing with investment properties first often frees up resources and clarity for the bigger conversation about your home.

So what exactly are we looking at? Let us walk you through two evaluation tools, starting with your home.

FOR YOUR HOME: FIVE THINGS TO FACE

1. HEALTH—PERSONAL WELL-BEING AND QUALITY OF LIFE

Start with this: "How's my home working for me? Does it fulfill the current quality of life that I desire?" Rate each one and be honest with yourself because if your well-being declines, your home isn't supporting you anymore.

2. HOME SAFETY AND SUITABILITY

Ask yourself: "Do I feel safe in my home? Does my home support aging with dignity?" Really think about it. The stairs you've climbed for thirty years—how much longer can you manage them? What about the bathroom? The yard work that used to take an afternoon now takes all weekend. And how far are you from your kids and medical care?

When your home stops fitting your life, staying can be dangerous.

3. FAMILY SUPPORT AND CAREGIVER CAPACITY

Love doesn't equal ability. Your kids might love you with everything they have, but if they live three states away or work sixty hours a week, how can they realistically help?

How often can they actually show up? For how long? And what happens when you need more than they can give? We've seen caregiver burnout destroy families because the adult children care too much and can't do it all.

4. FINANCIAL STRATEGY AND REAL ESTATE PLANNING

Let's talk numbers. Do you have long-term care insurance? How much? Life insurance? What's your home actually worth in today's market? More importantly, how much equity could you unlock if you needed to?

Some people want to preserve everything for their heirs, while others need the money to live. There's no right answer, but you need to know your options.

5. FUTURE NEEDS AND TIMING

Timing is a big topic. Would you like to make the decision about where and when your next move will be, or would you like to let someone else make that decision for you?

Think ten or twenty years out. If you can't make decisions for yourself, who do you want to make them? Have you talked to that person about it?

FOR INVESTMENT PROPERTIES: GETTING CLEAR ON THE NUMBERS

Investment properties are different. They should be the easiest part of the conversation. There's no childhood bedroom or family story, just numbers that tell the truth.

But this is where families often freeze, because they attach emotion to something that was never meant to be emotional.

1. WHAT'S YOUR GOAL?

First thing we ask: "Do you need the income to sustain the life you desire?"

If the answer is yes, then every decision should focus on maximizing cash flow. If it's no, then we look at other options. Maybe you want to bless a loved one, or you may want passive income that won't create family fights. Whichever route you take, you have to know your goal first.

2. WHAT'S KEEPING YOU STUCK?

People tell themselves stories. They say things like:

"My parents said never sell this property."

"I don't want to pay taxes on the gain,"

"I'm not losing money,"

"I have a good tenant."

But what's more important, keeping your tenant comfortable or keeping your family together after you're gone? You get to decide what matters most to you. Many don't do anything because it's easier not to change anything and therefore become philanthropists as opposed to investors.

3. THE PAIN AND BURDEN YOU'RE CARRYING

Rate these situations from 1-5 (1 = no stress, 5 = keeps me up at night). How much stress do these cause you?

- Dealing with tenants

- Maintaining properties

- Rising taxes and insurance costs

- Major repairs you know are coming

- Worrying about your kids fighting over these properties

Look at where you scored 4 or 5. These are the properties, or the aspects of ownership, that deserve your attention first.

For each high-stress item, ask yourself: What would need to change for this to become a 2? Write that down.

What many people don't calculate is the stress cost. You can measure the money, but what's your peace of mind worth?

4. THE PATH IS IN THE MATH

We run three simple analyses:

- Asset Performance Test: How is this property performing?

- Capitalization Rate Analysis: What's your return?

- Cash-on-Cash Analysis if there's debt involved.

When you're doing all the work of being a landlord but earning less than a passive investment would give you, it might be time to consider a change. We all tell ourselves stories about why we keep properties, but the path is in the math, and most haven't considered the impact of what improved cash flow improvements could do for them.

5. YOU HAVE MORE OPTIONS THAN YOU THINK

Most folks think they're stuck, they have to either keep the property or take the tax hit because that's what they've been told. But it's not the whole story.

You could do a 1031 exchange for better cash flow, exchange to a different market where returns are higher, upgrade to a better property, divide properties among family members while you're alive to see how they handle it, or exchange into a DST for passive income. The options exist; you just need to know about them. And sometimes, learning about these options feels better when you can see how they've unfolded in real life for others.

STORIES OF TAKING THE FIRST STEP

Seeing others' journeys can make your own path clearer. These are real families who sat in our office, stuck in the same place you might be right now. Some waited too long, while others acted just in time. All of them teach us something about the power of asking that first question.

THE INVESTMENT PROPERTY WAKE-UP CALL

A stressed friend and past client called us a while ago. She had a tenant for years, she was collecting rent, but there was no formal agreement.

When the original tenant left, he said, "My friend will pay you." There was no paperwork involved, only a handshake. It turns out that the friend paid once, then stopped, leading her to learn that people she'd never even met were living in her property.

She was so afraid of confrontation, she hadn't visited the property in months. The neighbors told her they heard the tenants talking about guns and ammunition. Now she was afraid to go to her own property.

The sheriff couldn't help because they wouldn't answer the door and therefore he couldn't serve their formal eviction notice. For two months, she lived in high anxiety with no rent coming in, property damage piling up, and was afraid to confront them due to her concern for her safety.

All because the easy route, doing nothing, seemed simpler than facing hard decisions.

When we finally helped her resolve it, she had one clear thought: "I never want to own rental property again."

We helped her do a 1031 exchange into a DST (Delaware Statutory Trust). Now she makes more income than she ever did as a landlord. While she has zero tenant headaches now, it took hitting rock bottom for her to ask that first question: "What am I really trying to accomplish with this property?"

THE POWER OF ASKING "WHAT IF?"

Another couple came in with four properties. All profitable, but not generating much income—about 2% returns.

We asked her, "What would you do with more income?"

Her eyes lit up. He said, "I'm sixty-seven, and I've never really traveled. That's my dream."

We ran the numbers, and by repositioning her properties through a 1031 exchange, we could generate an additional $32,000 a year.

She looked at us with tears in her eyes and said, "That's more than travel money. That's my life. You're giving me my life."

All it took was asking one question: "If you could make more money from these properties, would you?"

THE COUPLE WHO GOT IT RIGHT

Not every story we use as an example features a crisis. One of our clients, a couple, had been talking about moving to a retirement community for years. The husband had cancer, and his health was declining. But instead of waiting, the husband and wife sold their five-bedroom house and moved into a community where she could live independently while he received the care he needed, all in the same building.

Now they see each other every day. She has her social life and independence and he has the support his health requires. Neither carries the burden of maintaining a house that no longer fits their life.

This couple pruned away what no longer served them, and everything else blossomed. They're living a different life, but it's the right life for this season.

Why? Because they asked the question while they still had the power to answer it.

YOUR MOVE

Every family that successfully navigated these decisions has one thing in common: Someone dared to ask the first question.

The questions are here, and these stories show you what's possible. The only thing missing is your decision to begin.

Take a breath, pick up a pen, and ask yourself the question you've been avoiding.

Your family's future starts with that single act of courage.

YOUR WAKE-UP CALL QUESTIONS

Before moving to the next chapter, answer these questions honestly:

For Everyone

1. What question about your future have you been avoiding?

2. What would change if you had complete clarity about your real estate plans?

3. Who in your family would benefit most from you creating a plan?

For Homeowners

1. On a scale of 1-5, how much purpose, routine, and joy do you have where you live? (1 = very little, 5 = my home supports my life fully)

If you scored 3 or below, ask yourself: What's missing? Is it connection with others? Activities that give you purpose? A layout that works for how you live now? Write down one thing that would raise your score.

2. Can your home accommodate your needs if your health changes?

3. Do you want to choose when and where you move, or let circumstances decide?

FOR INVESTMENT PROPERTY OWNERS

1. Are your properties generating the income you need?

2. What's the real cost—emotional and financial—of maintaining the status quo?

3. If you could make more money with less stress, would you?

THE MOST IMPORTANT QUESTION

Are you ready to stop letting fear make your decisions?

If you answered yes, you're ready for the next step. You know the questions now, but asking them is just the beginning. In the next chapter, you'll understand what else needs to be in place—being honest with yourself about aging, imagining the life you want in ten or twenty years, understanding your financial picture, and knowing your options.

It all starts with the courage to face what is, so you can create what could be.

The choice, as always, is yours.

CHAPTER 10
Your Proactive Checklist

We have a friend who had a heart attack. When we heard he was going to have heart surgery, we immediately pictured the doctors cutting open his chest and putting him back together. We thought he would be in the hospital for weeks.

But thankfully, that grim reality is not what happened.

Our dear friend went into the hospital where doctors put a tiny hole in his vein, ran a wire up to his heart, inserted a stent—basically a balloon—to open the valve, pulled it out, and he walked out that same day.

Technology is going to keep our bodies alive longer than we ever imagined. The problem we're going to have doesn't have to do with our bodies, but our *minds*. There hasn't been much doctors can do about memory challenges yet, and that's why being proactive is important.

Many of us are in denial. We think we'll remain the way we are today for the rest of our lives. We want to talk about the past because it's comfortable. But talking about the future is the conversation your family needs you to have. The future of maybe not being able to walk or being unable to recognize loved ones is a possible reality that people don't want to picture as they get older. So naturally, humans think, "I'll think of a plan later. I don't need to worry about it now."

But as you've learned in the previous nine chapters, the ones who acknowledge the reality of getting older and take action are the ones who keep their families together, avoid being a burden, and turn wealth into a legacy.

By now, you understand the risks of staying reactive—the family disputes, tax consequences, burden on your children—and you know the

PLAN framework, but knowing isn't enough. So what makes people take action?

Moving forward doesn't require smarts (remember the story about the CPA and her attorney daughter?); it requires being proactive.

See, most people live a passive life. They just take life day by day, avoiding the thought of what's ahead in the long run. That's why when we ask people, "Do you have a real estate plan?" Very few say yes.

In this chapter, we're going to break down ten essential pieces that you need to have in place in order to be proactive. Some pieces will deal with your home, and some will deal with your investment properties. We will cover the details of the hard conversation topics we started talking about in the previous chapter, like your health, death, and who's going to get what.

Once you know exactly what needs to happen, those tough conversations can become manageable, and you can move from reactive to proactive.

In chapter 9, you started asking yourself the hard questions. Now we're going to show you what to do with the answers.

Let's start with your home.

YOUR HOME: FIVE THINGS THAT NEED TO HAPPEN

STOP THINKING ABOUT IT AND START DOING IT

When some people read about being proactive, they may nod their heads or even tell their spouse, "We should really do something about this." Then months, and sometimes, years go by, but not much changes. Knowing and committing to change are two different things. This is why people often don't change.

The first step is to make the decision that you're going to be *proactive* about your home starting today, even if it doesn't feel like the perfect time. As we say to our clients, "You're either proactive or reactive. There's no in-between."

ACTION STEP

Schedule a two-hour block on your calendar this week labeled "Real Estate Planning." This is protected time for you (and your spouse, if applicable) to work through the exercises in this chapter.

PICTURE YOURSELF AT EIGHTY-FIVE (EVEN IF YOU DON'T WANT TO)

Should you be blessed to live long enough, you're going to need some level of help.

In chapter 9, we talked about facing the reality that one day we'll need help. But it's one thing to say, "Yeah, I know," and another to actually imagine what that moment might look like. Most people don't want to picture themselves needing support because it's uncomfortable. But leaning into that discomfort is how we protect the people we love.

But, if you can't imagine it, how can you plan for it?

The medical reality we talked about earlier means your body will likely outlive your independence. Technology keeps us going, but it can't prevent memory challenges, and that's why we're advocates for people being in community with others instead of living alone.

In our experience, isolation is one of the biggest challenges of aging. It creates a lack of cerebral stimulation when your mind needs to be constantly moving through activity and conversations with others. You need people who challenge you, make you laugh, and help you remember why Tuesday is different from Wednesday.

Most of our clients tell us they can't picture themselves at eighty-five or ninety. They still see themselves as they are today. But when we start asking questions like, "How did your parents age? What kind of help did they need? And if you could rewrite that story for yourself, what would you want to be different?" the picture starts to come into focus. Suddenly, they can see it. And once they can see it, they can plan for it.

ACTION STEP

Write down three specific scenarios: what you'll need at eighty, eighty-five, and ninety. Be specific to avoid saying only the word "help." Help with what? Groceries? Driving? Getting medications? Bathing? The more detailed your imagination, the better your plan can be. Look at your own parents or others you've known and think about what they needed that they didn't plan for.

DECIDE WHAT YOUR NEXT CHAPTER LOOKS LIKE

Now that you've committed to being proactive and imagined yourself needing help, it's time to have clarity on what kind of life you want to live in the next ten or twenty years. Rather than only accepting that you'll age, you want to decide what that life looks like.

If you're seventy now, what does eighty look like? If you're slowing down at eighty, you might need help going to the bathroom, cooking food, or taking a bath. The question is: Who's going to help you? Where will you be? Who do you want around you? What kind of environment supports the life you desire?

Creating your ten-to-twenty year vision is about having acceptance and awareness of where your mind, body, and faculties are going, followed by creating a plan for the life you want anyway.

Be the proactive person who says, "I know I'm going to get older and need help, so I'm going to make the move now while I can. Under my terms, and when my spouse is around me. We're going to do this together."

By taking action on your next living situation, you and your spouse can end up in a community where you get physical, mental, social, and even spiritual support. It's the holistic approach to aging.

ACTION STEP

Get specific about your ten-to-twenty year vision. Where will you live? What support will you have? Will you be in a community or at home? Who's around you? Don't just think "somewhere nice," but give details about the place, people, and daily rhythm.

DO THE MATH NOW

In chapter 7, we talked about the Assets pillar of the PLAN framework. Now it's time to get specific about how your home fits into your financial reality, as this is where most people have a blind spot.

They know their Social Security, maybe their 401(k), but they don't connect their biggest asset, which is their home, to their retirement plan. It's like having a million dollars in the bank but forgetting it exists when you're figuring out if you can afford something.

If you've lived in your home for two out of the last five years, the federal government gives you a gift through IRC Section 121. You can take $250,000 of the gain out of the sale tax-free. For a married couple, that's $500,000 tax-free. This is one of the greatest tax benefits we have as homeowners.

The catch is, if you move out and wait more than three years to sell, you lose this benefit completely. Your home becomes an investment property subject to capital gains tax. We've seen people lose thousands of dollars simply because they didn't know about this timeline.

The real question becomes: How are you going to pay for senior living that might cost $6,000 to $10,000 per month? Do you have enough monthly income, or will you need to tap into your home equity? And if you need that equity, can you access some of it tax-free?

ACTION STEP

Calculate three critical numbers:

1. your home's current value and how much tax-free money you could access if you sell within the IRC 121 timeline,

2. your total monthly income from all sources, and

3. the cost of care in your area

When you calculate these three numbers, you'll know whether your plan works mathematically. Do the math now so you're not doing it during a crisis.

WALK THROUGH THE DOORS BEFORE YOU NEED TO

If you've never walked into a retirement community, it can be hard to move to one.

We're advocates for visiting retirement communities before you need one because you can't make an informed decision about something you've never seen.

Today's senior living options are not like what your parents experienced, but until you walk through those doors, you won't know that.

Maybe you think that you'll live with your kids, and while that is a valid thought, we need to talk about this situation honestly. Living with your kids can bring a whole bag of issues. If there's more than one child, the one who provides care is going to think they deserve more of the inheritance. Maybe they do, or maybe they don't, but now you've created dissension in the family.

In a retirement community, nobody is obligated or responsible for you outside of the staff, so there's no resentment in the family. The kids can visit because they want to, not because they have to. That's why we're fans of retirement communities, as they preserve relationships.

ACTION STEP

Visit three senior living options in the next sixty days. Take the tour, eat lunch there, and talk to residents. Don't worry about committing to anything because you're there to educate yourself about what's available. And if you're considering living with your kids, try it out first by spending a month with them. See how it feels for everyone involved.

YOUR PROPERTIES: FIND OUT WHAT YOU OWN

Now let's shift to your investment properties. If you don't live in your property, it's an asset, and assets need to perform. So let's see what your assets (or potential assets) are truly doing.

WAKE UP TO WHAT YOU'RE SITTING ON

When people come to us, they often don't know what their investment properties are doing for them, and that's completely understandable. Sometimes the property was inherited from Mom and Dad, while other times, it was bought so long ago that the details have gotten fuzzy. They see it as "the house where little Johnny lives" or "Mom's old place."

But as you've seen throughout the pages of this book, once you start seeing your investment properties as wealth that hasn't been unlocked yet, you start asking different questions.

Together with a Real Estate Wealth Advisor, you'll want to discover four specific numbers for each property:

- What is it worth today?

- What is your cost basis? (What you originally paid, or the value when you inherited it.)

- What's your capital gains tax if you sold it? (That's the amount you keep when you do a 1031 exchange.)

- How hard is your property working for you? (That's your cap rate.)

The goal is to be confident in your knowledge of how your properties are performing, instead of only being able to say the address and who lives there.

ACTION STEP

Consider connecting with a real estate wealth advisor to help you understand what your properties are doing, so you know your choices.

MATCH YOUR GOAL TO YOUR STRATEGY

In chapter 9, you figured out whether you need income from your properties. Now that you know your numbers, we can match your goal to a specific strategy.

If you realized that you need income and your properties are underperforming, the questions become: When should I start making more money? How do we get there? Am I comfortable with properties in different markets? What's my risk tolerance?

If you don't need the income and you're thinking about your family, the questions shifts: How do you want to bless them? Through properties they can use now? Maybe passive income that won't burden them with management? Or possibly, through maximizing the total value, even if it means more complexity?

Each "how" leads to a different path. Income-seekers might move into multi-family units in growing markets, those wanting simplicity might choose DSTs, and families focused on blessing children might acquire properties near where the kids live.

ACTION STEP

Now that you know what your properties are worth and what they're earning, write down your specific goal:

- "I want to generate $______ more per month,"

- "I want to help my daughter buy a home in Denver,"

- "I want to remove the burden of owning the property but keep earning income."

Create your specific goals so that they lead to specific solutions.

CALCULATE WHAT FEAR IS COSTING YOU

By now, you know what you have and what you want. Now let's move into what's at stake with the decisions you're facing.

Remember those tax rates we mentioned? Say you have a property worth $1 million that you bought for $300,000. That's $700,000 in gains, which is great. You did well, but that gain comes with a bigger bill than you'd expect.

First, there's the capital gains tax, which is 20% federal plus 3.8% if your adjusted gross income is over $400,000, plus whatever your state charges. If you've been depreciating this property on your taxes all these years, the government wants that back too. That's called depreciation recapture, and it's taxed at 25%.

Add it all up, and you could hand over $250,000 or more to the government on that million-dollar sale. That's money that could have stayed in your family.

Now, if that million-dollar property is only making you a 2% return, and you're keeping it just to avoid the tax bill, let's think about this differently. You're giving up potentially 3% more return every year, that's $30,000 annually, to avoid a one-time tax. Over ten years, that's $300,000 in lost income. See how the math changes when you look at the whole picture?

And when it comes to your family, the numbers make things even clearer. Real estate doesn't divide equally. If you have multiple properties and kids, someone's getting more than someone else. Or worse, they're all sharing properties they can't agree on.

The math never works out clean, as one property might have better cash flow, another might be in a better location, and the third might need major repairs. Who gets what? That impossible math is where family fights begin.

We believe there's a better way. Through strategies like 1031 exchanges, you can reposition that wealth without triggering those taxes. Just like through pre-inheritance planning, you can solve the division problem while you're here to guide the conversation.

ACTION STEP

Take those numbers you discovered about your properties and write down two things. First, if you sold today, what would you keep after taxes? Your tax advisor can help with this. Second, if you could reposition into something earning 5%, how much more income would that generate?

Then, write your children's names next to your properties. If you can't easily show who gets what fairly, you've discovered where a better plan is needed.

PICK THE OPTION THAT FITS YOU

Most people think they're trapped with only two choices: keep an underperforming property or pay massive taxes when they sell. Before we started on this journey, those were the options we were familiar with too. But there are actually several ways to reposition your wealth without the tax hit.

OPTION ONE: MAKE MORE MONEY

The question is, how much more? There's a risk-reward relationship here. If you want maximum returns, it's going to be riskier. For example, we have properties with 14% cap rates, but they're in areas where the land is cheap and the rents are high. You'll make more money, but you won't get much appreciation, and it's in a lower-valued area. Compare that to Hawaii, where you might get 5% at best.

OPTION TWO: EARN TRUE PASSIVE INCOME

Maybe you just want 5% return without any headaches. That's the DST, Delaware Statutory Trust, where you'll never get a phone call from a tenant, or have to repair a dishwasher or garbage disposal. It's like an annuity where money shows up every month, and you don't worry about anything.

OPTION THREE: BLESS YOUR FAMILY NOW

What do your kids and grandkids want? We can help you buy it, keep it in your name, and when you pass, or ensure that it goes straight to them through your trust. It's a pre-inheritance plan where they get what they need now, and you get to see their joy.

Each option serves a different purpose. One is about maximizing money, the second option helps you simplify your life, and the third supports you in taking care of your loved ones while you're here to guide them.

ACTION STEP

Which of these three speaks to you? Your first instinct usually tells you what matters most. Once you know that, we can get specific about how to make it happen.

FIND THE RIGHT PARTNER FOR YOUR JOURNEY

By now, you understand your properties, your goals, and your options. The last part is having someone who can help you make it happen.

This kind of real estate planning—1031 exchanges, DSTs, and pre-inheritance strategies—requires specialized knowledge. Most real estate professionals are wonderful at what they do, but they haven't been trained in these specific strategies.

A certified real estate wealth advisor understands the complexities we've been talking about. They know how to structure these transactions so you keep your wealth instead of losing it to taxes. More importantly, they'll ask questions to understand your unique situation rather than pushing a one-size-fits-all solution.

We know that sharing your financial details with a stranger makes you feel vulnerable. After all this reading and thinking, the idea of opening up about your properties, family dynamics, and fears about the future can make you hesitate. We understand because you're trusting someone with the decades of hard work, family relationships, and legacy you want to leave

ACTION STEP

Find a certified real estate wealth advisor and share what you've been thinking about. You'll know pretty quickly if they're the right fit. If they listen more than they talk, ask thoughtful questions about your family and your goals, and if you feel understood rather than sold to, that's your person. And if the first one doesn't feel right, that's okay too. Keep looking until you find someone who feels like a partner in this journey.

WHAT LIFE FEELS LIKE WHEN YOU HAVE A PLAN

When you have the ten pieces we just covered in place, you'll find peace of mind. The type of peace where your friends and family can tell that you're truly fine, and where you can have a restful night's sleep.

The feeling of significance and freedom will also come to the surface. Like the burden that's been sitting on your shoulders for years is gone. You can pass away knowing your kids won't fight, and that they'll be taken care of. As one of our clients said, "I can go anytime now. Not that I want to, but I'm ready."

You can also finally do those things you've been putting off, like traveling more and enjoying your life instead of worrying about it. When you're not stressed about your properties or lying awake wondering if you'll run out of money, you can start living.

Finally, you get to see the gratitude of the people you love. You'll cherish the moments when your daughter realizes she can afford that house where she's raising your grandchildren, or when your son understands he won't have to manage properties he never wanted. You'll remember the hugs and tears of relief.

These pieces give you a life where you're in control instead of your properties controlling you.

YOUR TEN-POINT CHECK

See where you stand by using this tool to help you see what needs attention.

FOR YOUR HOME

☐ I've made the decision to be proactive instead of thinking about it.

☐ I can picture myself at eighty, eighty-five, and ninety—and what help I'll need.

☐ I have a clear vision for where I want to live the next ten-to-twenty years.

☐ I know my home's value and understand the two-of-five year tax rule.

☐ I've visited at least one senior living option.

FOR YOUR INVESTMENT PROPERTIES

☐ I know the cap rate for each property I own.

☐ I've clarified whether I need income or want to bless my family.

☐ I've calculated my tax liability if I sold today.

☐ I understand my three options (higher returns, DST, family blessing).

☐ I know what kind of advisor I need, and I'm ready to call.

QUICK REALITY CHECK

If you checked fewer than five boxes, you're where most people are aware but not quite prepared yet, which is okay. Now you know what to work on.

If you checked five-to-eight boxes, you're making progress. Focus on filling the remaining gaps before life fills them for you.

If you checked nine-to-ten boxes, you're ready. The only thing left is to take action.

BEFORE YOU CLOSE THIS BOOK

After reading all of this, are you going to do something about it this week? If yes, write down exactly what that is: _______________________

If no, ask yourself what's stopping you. Fear? Confusion? Time? Whatever it is, that's what needs addressing first.

YOU DON'T HAVE TO FIGURE THIS OUT ALONE

Whatever you wrote on that line, or whatever's keeping you from writing anything at all, you don't have to navigate it by yourself.

Awareness is the first step to creating the legacy you desire. Now that you're aware, what will you do with that awareness? We'll be waiting for you at the Real Estate Wealth Hive, ready to help you take the next step. Because no one should have to figure this out alone.

If you're ready to go deeper with the PLAN framework and want ongoing support, consider joining our Real Estate Wealth Hive. When you join the hive, you'll get access to monthly Q&A calls with us, educational resources, and a community of both families and professionals working through these same challenges. Visit www.DanIhara.com to learn more.

Remember what we said in chapter 1, the best time to plant a tree was twenty years ago. The second-best time is now. Your family's real estate wealth journey starts with the decision to be proactive. Make that decision today.

SEVEN DAYS FROM NOW

The families who avoid becoming part of the 70% statistic that fight over real estate inheritance are the ones who pick up the phone and schedule that first appointment.

That blank line above where you wrote your commitment is the difference between your kids thanking you and your kids hiring attorneys.

Whatever you wrote on that line, making those calls, scheduling those tours, or getting those numbers, do it this week because every week you wait, you're choosing to stay reactive when you could be proactive.

The hard part was reading this far and facing the truth about what needs to happen.

You've already done the hard part.

CONCLUSION
Your Legacy Starts With Your Next Decision

Every morning, Julie and I watch the sunrise from our home in Hawaii. It's our daily reminder that each day brings new possibilities, new choices, and new opportunities to impact the people we love. As we write this final chapter together, we can't help but think about you, sitting there with this book in your hands, perhaps feeling overwhelmed by everything you've discovered.

We understand. You've just spent ten chapters facing hard truths about aging, family dynamics, and decisions you've been avoiding. Maybe you picked up this book because your adult child gave it to you, worried about your future. Or maybe you bought it yourself, knowing something needs to change but not knowing where to start.

The fact that you're still reading tells us you're ready to wake up.

THE JOURNEY YOU'VE JUST TAKEN

You read a book about real estate planning, but more importantly, you confronted questions most people spend their whole lives avoiding:

- You faced the reality that your home might not be safe forever, and that staying too long could cost you everything you've worked to build.

- You learned that 70% of families fight over real estate after parents pass away, and now you know it's preventable.

- You learned the hard lesson that good intentions aren't enough. When a trust says "my kids share everything equally" without explaining how, you're leaving them to figure out the impossible math of dividing what can't be divided.

- You saw through the myths that have kept you stuck, like "I'll figure it out when the time comes" or "My smart kids will handle it."

- You understand now that your investment properties aren't just houses with doors and windows, but wealth waiting to be unlocked, repositioned, and used for good.

- You've been given the PLAN framework, a way to think about Properties, Longevity, Assets, and Next Generation that brings clarity to chaos.

- You know the difference between being proactive and reactive, and what each choice costs your family.

- You have the questions that lead to answers, so that you finally stop spinning in circles.

But what we've learned from working with over 1,600 families is that you can read every page, understand every strategy, and still stay stuck if you don't take that first step.

Some people may close this book, set it on their nightstand, and tell themselves they'll do something about it "soon." They'll live another day, month, or year in that comfortable space between knowing and doing. Until one day, a fall, diagnosis, or a crisis forces their hand.

We believe you're different. You wouldn't have read this far if you weren't.

TRUTH—THIS WAS NEVER ABOUT REAL ESTATE

Julie and I are Christians, and we believe this life is temporary. The material things, like properties, money, and even the houses we're so attached to, will all rust and rot because they have no eternal value.

What *does* matter are relationships, family bonds, and the legacy of love you leave behind.

When you're gone, how do you want your kids to treat each other? Do you want your kids to love each other? Or do you want them hiring attorneys, fighting over properties, destroying relationships over things that won't matter in eternity?

The mission of this book has never been about real estate. Our goal has been to guide you in keeping your family together. Because while we're helping you create earthly plans for earthly things, there's a much bigger plan at work. And that plan values people more than property, relationships above real estate, and love before money.

MONEY IS GOOD FOR THE GOOD IT DOES

Gary Keller, our mentor, taught us that money is good for the good it does. The question is, what good do you want to do?

We had one client who loved puppies. We asked her, "You have so much money. What if you could build an organization that takes care of pets?" Her eyes lit up like we'd given her permission to dream for the first time in decades.

We're inviting you to make a shift here. You've spent your whole life in scarcity mode, but what if you could live from abundance? Instead of hoarding, what if you became someone who blesses others? And what would it look like to stop passively existing and begin living with intention?

You can't take things with you. So what good can it do between now and when you leave this planet?

YOUR IMMEDIATE NEXT STEPS

We're not going to leave you wondering what to do next. Here's where to start:

THIS MONTH

Visit the Real Estate Wealth Hive at www. DanIhara.com. We've created a community where consumers and professionals come together to learn, share, and support each other. You'll find:

- free self-assessment tools to understand where you stand,

- worksheets to calculate cap rates and tax consequences,

- educational resources about 1031 exchanges and DSTs, and

- connection to certified Real Estate Wealth Advisors who understand our approach.

THIS QUARTER

Make the big decision: Are you going to stay reactive, or become proactive? If you choose to be proactive, commit to creating your real estate plan. Whether you do it yourself with our tools or work with an advisor, the key is to start.

OUR PROMISE TO YOU

Twenty years ago, we started this journey thinking we were in the real estate business. We learned we're actually in the family preservation business. Every strategy, tool, and question we've shared in this book serves one mission: keeping families together while helping them build, protect, and pass on wealth.

This book exists because you, your family, and the legacy you leave matters.

Remember, you have the wisdom to recognize when change is needed, and you have the love for your family that makes all of this worth doing.

Welcome to your new beginning, the life you were meant to live.

With hope, faith, and anticipation for your journey ahead,

Dan and Julie Ihara

YOUR NEXT STEP

You have the questions. You have the framework. Now it's time to put it into action.

We created a free training that walks you through your first steps — so you don't have to do this alone. It's the bridge between reading this book and making your plan real.

Scan below or visit free.danihara.com

ABOUT THE AUTHORS

DAN IHARA

Dan Ihara is one of the most trusted voices in America on real estate, aging, and generational wealth. For more than two decades, he has sat at thousands of kitchen tables, guiding families through some of the most emotional and financially significant decisions of their lives.

Dan quickly discovered that traditional real estate was failing families at the very moment they needed the most support. Selling a home or managing investment property was the intersection of memory, money, fear, family, and future. So Dan built a different model.

Instead of pushing advice, he leads families through a question-based approach that creates clarity, reveals blind spots, and empowers them to make confident, informed decisions. His guiding belief is simple: "When you ask better questions, families make better decisions."

This discovery-driven method has helped more than 1,600 families build, protect, and pass on real estate wealth without unnecessary taxes or painful family disputes. Dan has achieved a 100% success rate on over four hundred 1031 exchanges, and his strategies have helped families defer more than $112 million in capital gains taxes, keeping wealth in the family where it belongs.

Dan is the creator of the Build, Protect, Pass-On Real Estate Wealth methodology, now recognized nationally as a compassionate, holistic framework for serving aging families with dignity, wisdom, and strategy. He has been honored by the National Association of REALTORS ® with the Senior Real Estate Specialist Outstanding Service Award and has been one of Hawaii's Top 100 REALTORS ® for 19 years.

As the co-founder of KW Real Estate Planner, Dan trains thousands of agents nationwide on his client-first, planning-based methodology. Through his national speaking and education programs, he continues to change the way real estate professionals show up, and change the way families experience the biggest transitions of their lives.

Dan, the youngest of six, grew up under the loving guidance of his parents, the late Col. Les S. Ihara and Shirley Ihara. They gave him a priceless gift: the chance to see the world and learn from it. By age fourteen, he had traveled through forty states and lived in multiple countries, discovering along the way that people everywhere, despite different backgrounds, share common dreams, values, and beliefs.

Dan says, "I have two goals in life: To see every sunset and sunrise until I die, and to surf every day until I can't." He enjoys traveling with his family and takes his boys surfing to Mexico three times a year.

JULIE IHARA

Julie was born and raised in Hawaii, where her love for people and her entrepreneurial spirit showed up early, selling baked goods at makeshift neighborhood cookie stands and handcrafted jewelry at craft fairs. After an eighteen-year career in banking, where she led teams, developed client-care programs, and learned the power of relationships, she felt called to a deeper purpose: helping families through real estate.

In 2006, Julie and Dan built the Ihara Team with a mission to honor God by serving others with the highest level of competency, care, and compassion with uncompromised integrity. Their team quickly became one of Hawaii's Top 100 REALTORS ® for nearly two decades and was recognized as one of the state's "Fastest 50" growing companies. Along the way, they created service-driven businesses such as HI Property Management, Senior Move Managers, and their nonprofit Silver Spoons, all designed to support seniors and families in meaningful ways.

Julie finds deep purpose in serving seniors and families facing transition, and helping them move forward with grace, confidence, and peace. Her financial background and decades of experience allow her to guide families thoughtfully as they make important decisions and plan for the future with their investment properties. More importantly, she shares Dan's mission of keeping families together.

Her personal experiences with caring for her mom and advocating for her care have given her perspective and empathy for those going through this process. Julie's financial expertise, combined with her heart for service, helps families navigate the complex intersection of wealth transition and family dynamics.

Beyond business, Julie pours into her community. She serves at Pearlside Church in prayer ministry and mentorship, and she supports local families through her work with the Fukunaga Foundation and Scholarship Committee.

Julie and Dan have been happily married for thirty-five years and have three sons: Michael, James, and

Randy. Their greatest joy is their family, and they give all glory to Jesus Christ for the blessings in their life.

Together, Dan and Julie bring complementary expertise, his real estate planning strategies and her financial wisdom, united by their shared faith and commitment to preserving family relationships while building generational wealth.

CONNECT WITH DAN & JULIE

We'd love to continue this conversation with you. Scan below for free training and professionals who can support you in your journey to building and protecting your wealth.

free.danihara.com

ACKNOWLEDGMENTS

FROM DAN—

This book is the result of a lifetime of experiences, thousands of conversations around kitchen tables, and the grace of many people who have shaped my heart, my work, and my purpose.

First, I thank God for the wisdom, strength, and calling to serve families through the seasons of aging, transition, and legacy. Every insight in these pages comes from His guidance and the people He placed on my path.

To my parents, Col. Les S. Ihara and Shirley Ihara—thank you for teaching me the power of learning through experience and the importance of showing up with compassion. The travels, the lessons, the discipline, and the love you poured into me continue to guide every step I take. Even in your absence, your influence is alive in this work.

To my brothers and sisters, thank you for being my first community and for shaping the humility, grit, and faith that I carry into the world.

To my wife, Julie—my partner in every sense of the word. Your steady faith, unwavering support, and shared conviction to serve families have made this mission possible. You are the heart behind everything we do.

To our children, thank you for giving meaning to the word "legacy." You are the reason I care so deeply about helping families build, protect, and pass on what matters most.

FROM JULIE—

All glory to God.

Thank you to my parents, who are now in heaven, for instilling in me perseverance, independent thinking, kindness, humor, and creativity.

To my sibbies, Fukunaga Ohana, Ihara Ohana, Work Ohana, and dear friends—your love, support, wisdom, and prayers have carried me farther than you know.

To Dan, my best friend and partner in life, and to Mike, James, and Randy—you are my joy, my big why, and my motivation to leave the world better for you, your children, and your children's children.

Hugs to you all.

FROM DAN AND JULIE—

To the 1,600+ families who allowed us into your homes and trusted us with your stories, your fears, and your hopes—you are the true teachers of this book. Every chapter carries the imprint of your courage and vulnerability. Thank you for letting us walk alongside you.

To the incredible professionals who have partnered with us— REALTORS ® , CPAs, attorneys, trust officers, senior care specialists, and financial planners—thank you for believing in a better way to serve aging families. Your collaboration is proof that when we ask better questions, we create better outcomes.

To the agents, leaders, and students of the KW Real Estate Planner community: Your hunger to grow, to serve, and to change how our industry supports families inspires us every day. This movement exists because of your willingness to show up differently.

To our closest friends and mentors—thank you for the encouragement, the accountability, and the belief that this message needed to be shared with the world.

To Colette Ching Kazadzis, thank you for introducing us to Keller Williams and Gary Keller. You have changed our lives in so many ways. You've taught us how to work with a variety of people in a caring and compassionate way. Your love and support will forever be etched in our hearts.

TO GARY KELLER,

Thank you for being the spark behind this book and the guiding influence behind the work we do every day. Your leadership has shaped not only our business, but our understanding of what it truly means to serve families with wisdom, clarity, and purpose.

You taught us that real estate is far more than a career, it's a calling. You showed us that the right questions can change a person's life, that contribution matters more than production, and that true leadership is anchored in service.

Your vision challenged us to think bigger and dig deeper. You inspired us to transform the conversations we were having at kitchen tables into a framework that could help families everywhere. This book exists because you encouraged us to elevate our role from agents to advisors, from doers to teachers, from professionals to stewards of generational wealth.

Gary, the impact you have made on our lives and the families we serve is immeasurable. Your mentorship, your belief in what's possible, and your unwavering commitment to raising the standard of this industry gave us the courage to write these pages.

From the bottom of our hearts—thank you for inspiring this work.

And finally, to the reader: Thank you for picking up this book. Our hope is that the questions within these pages bring clarity, peace, and confidence to your family. If this book helps even one family avoid conflict, unnecessary taxes, or painful decisions, then every moment spent writing it was worthwhile.

This book is dedicated to the families who want to do the right thing, even when the path is unclear. You are not alone. We are honored to walk with you.